THE BAGH CAVES

THE BAGH CAVES
IN
THE GWALIOR STATE

Sir John Marshall, M.B. Garde,
Dr. J.Ph. Vogel, E.B. Havell,
Dr. James H. Cousins

SHUBHI PUBLICATIONS
GURGAON — INDIA

Published by
SHUBHI PUBLICATIONS
240, City Centre, M.G. Road
Gurgaon - 122 002.
Haryana, India

First Indian Edition - 2009

Published by Sanjay Arya for Shubhi Publications and *Printed in India*

Originally Published

THE BAGH CAVES

IN

THE GWALIOR STATE

Published by the India Society
in co-operation with
The Department of Archaeology, Gwalior
for
HIS LATE HIGHNESS
MAHARAJA SIR MADHAV RAO
SCINDIA ALIJAH BAHADUR
G.C.S.I., G.C.V.O., G.B.E., A.D.C.,
D.C.L., LL.D.

With Text by
Sir John Marshall, M. B. Garde, Dr. J. Ph. Vogel,
E. B. Havell, Dr. James H. Cousins,
together with a Forward by Laurence Binyon.

THE INDIA SOCIETY, 3 VICTORIA STREET, LONDON, S.W. 1.

1927

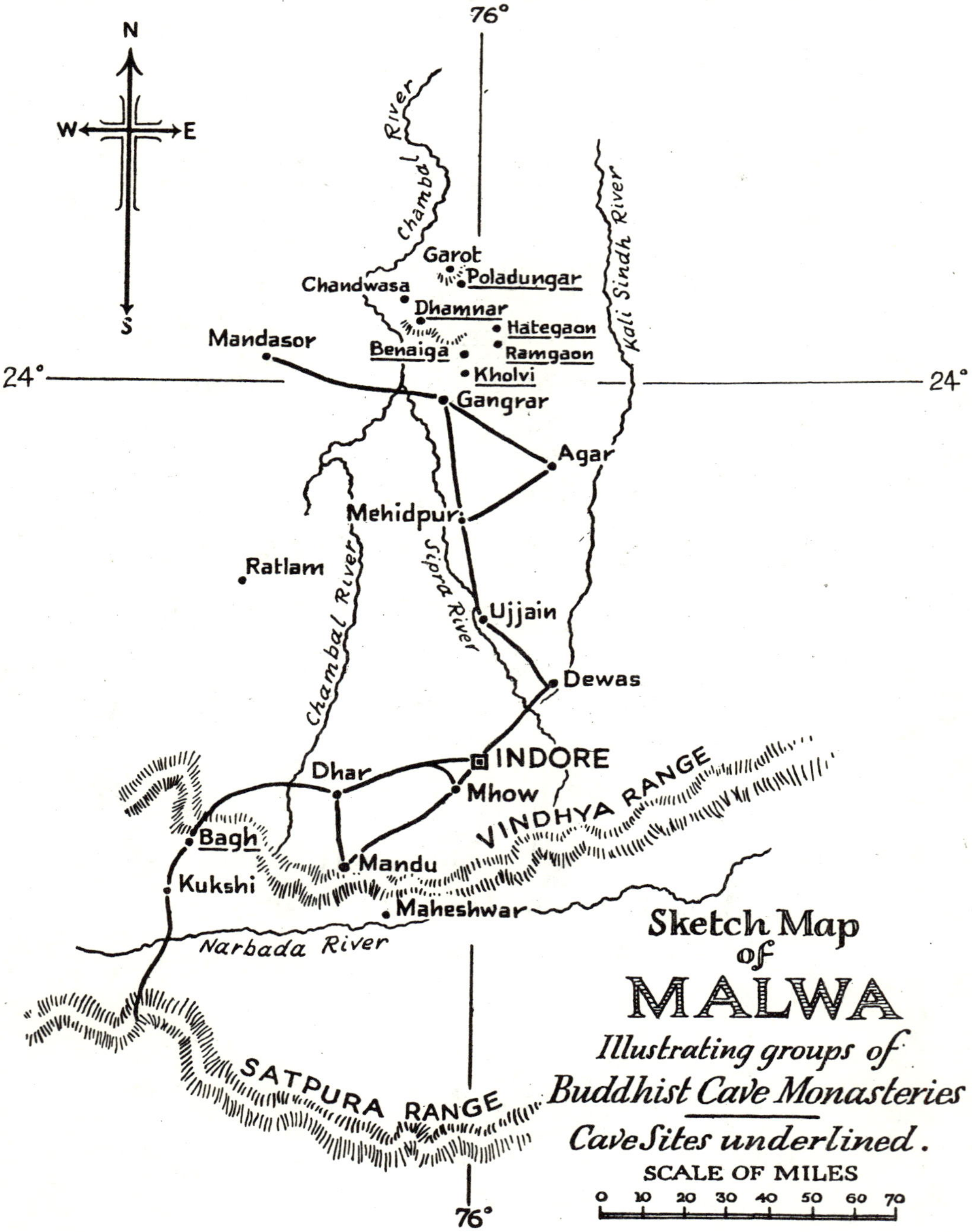

The India Society

CONTENTS.

LIST OF ILLUSTRATIONS.

DRAWINGS AND PLANS.

LIST OF ILLUSTRATIONS—*continued.*

DRAWINGS AND PLANS—*continued.*

COLOURED PLATES.

PREFACE

The India Society is deeply indebted to his late Highness Sir Madhav Rao Scindia of Gwalior, and to the late Lieut.-Colonel Charles Eckford Luard, for the preparation of this book. It was during Colonel Luard's residence in Gwalior that the late Maharajah planned with him to have the splendid, but at that time scarcely-known, frescoes at Bāgh copied by Indian artists. Their desire to have these copies reproduced and published in a volume by the India Society, which had already issued *Ajanta Frescoes*, is now fulfilled: but they have not lived to see the publication which they had so much at heart.

His Highness spared no expense in having the copies made with the utmost care. He graciously consented to their exhibition in the British Museum during the autumn of 1925, when their beauty and high importance were universally recognized.

These few lines were to have been written by Colonel Luard, who in his modesty wished that the text of this volume should be contributed by other writers, and that only a prefatory word should be added by himself, though without him the book would never have appeared. The preface remained unwritten; for Colonel Luard died, after a brief illness, on 17th May. At the request of my fellow-members of the Committee of the Society, I write these lines in homage to the memory of these two great lovers of Indian art, to commemorate our loss and to record our gratitude.

LAURENCE BINYON.

June, 1927.

THE CAVES OF BAGH

By SIR JOHN MARSHALL, Kt., C.I.E., Litt. D.

Of the whole vast galaxy of monuments that Antiquity has bequeathed to India, none are more remarkable or more interesting to the archæologist than her rock-hewn shrines and monasteries. Starting in the 3rd century B.C. and extending down to the 15th century A.D., they unfold for us the story of Indian architecture and art during those sixteen hundred years with a wealth of detail which more perishable buildings could never have preserved. Some are the work of the Buddhists, others of the Brahmans, and others of the Jains. Most are hollowed out, like caves, from the sides of cliffs and exhibit only the internal features of the structural prototypes from which they were copied ; a few, however, like the Kailasa at Ellora, and the Seven Pagodas at Mahavallipur, are hewn entire from the rock and are thus complete replicas of free standing edifices, finished in every particular both without and within. In many of the earlier examples the spirit of imitation is so strong that every feature of the original, even to the nail-heads of the wooden timbering, has been sedulously reproduced in the stone, while in some cases actual wooden ribbing, though quite superfluous for structural purposes, has nevertheless been inserted beneath the vaulted roofs. This painstaking care on the part of the excavators has naturally given a special value to these monolithic monuments— a value that is all the greater because time and decay have spared relatively few of the contemporary buildings from which they were copied. This, however, is by no means their only claim to distinction; they are the repositories of an almost endless array of sculpture, including some of the finest examples of Indian plastic art, and, what is perhaps even more important, they have preserved to us the sole surviving examples of ancient Indian wall-paintings. These paintings, it is true, are not numerous. They are found in only three groups of Cave Temples: at Ajanta in the Northern Dekhan, at Bagh in Central India, and at Sigiri in Ceylon, and all of them, without exception, have suffered severely at the hand of time. Mutilated, however, and faded as they are, they still constitute a priceless treasure, which no pains or expense should be deemed too great to save for posterity. That any paintings at all should have escaped effacement in the tropical climate of India is to be accounted a stroke of rare good fortune: still more fortunate is it that most of those paintings should belong to the Golden Age of Indian Art. How much would the world not give for such samples of the painting of Classic Greece? Yet it may well be doubted if the paintings even of Polygnotus or Zeuxis would have been more illuminating for the general history of Art, than the paintings of Ajanta and Bagh. For the school which these paintings represent was the source and fountain head from which half the art of Asia drew its inspiration, and no one can study their rhythmic composition, their instinctive beauty of line, the majestic grace of their figures, and the boundless wealth of their decorative imagery without realising what a far-reaching influence they exerted on the art, not of India alone and her colonies, but of every other country to which the religion of the Buddha penetrated. Nor are these paintings to be appraised only in relation to the art in Asia. They will bear comparison with the best that Europe could produce down to the time of Michael Angelo. This is a strong statement, no doubt, to make and one which many may be disposed at first sight to challenge. Nevertheless, it is the considered opinion of perhaps the greatest living authority on Italian fresco painting. I refer to Signor A. Cecconi, the expert who has carried out the work of conserving the Ajanta paintings, and it has been fully endorsed by many another eminent critic. Enough, however, has already been said to give the reader an idea of the unique value attaching to these Cave temples, and of the art treasures contained in them, and we may turn now to the particular group which forms the subject of this monograph.

The Caves of Bagh have already been made known to the public by three descriptive articles: the first by Lieutenant Dangerfield in the *Transactions of the Literary Society of Bombay*;[1] the second by Dr. E. Impey in the *Journal of the Bombay Branch of the Royal Asiatic Society*;[2] and the third by Colonel C. E. Luard in the *Indian Antiquary*.[3] The last mentioned is, as the author himself states, largely a repetition of Dr. Impey's article, improved upon and modified where necessary, and illustrated by a useful series of photographs and plans, which had been lacking in the earlier accounts. Since Colonel Luard described the caves much has been done by Mr. Garde and the archæological staff of the Gwalior State to clear them of fallen débris and save them from further decay; and as a result of these measures the fresh plans and sections which accompany this monograph have the advantage of being more detailed and accurate than it was then possible to make

(1) Vol. II, pp. 206-14. (2) Vol. V, pp. 543-73. (3) Vol. XXXIX, pp. 225, sqq.

them. Still more striking is the advance made by Mr. A. K. Haldar and his colleagues in the copying of the wall paintings. Seeing, indeed, how faded and fragile the originals now are, it may safely be predicted that they are never again likely to be copied with greater fidelity and skill than these artists have brought to bear upon their task. Yet, if the earlier copies were not as perfect as they might have been, let it not be forgotten that it was due to Colonel Luard's efforts that steps have since been taken to secure a more reliable record of these priceless relics, and that but for the interest which he aroused the present monograph would probably never have been written.

The Caves of Bagh[(1)]—so called from the neighbouring village of that name—are situated among the southern slopes of the Vindhya hills in what is now the Amjhera district of the Gwalior State. The cliff side in which they are excavated rises some 150 feet above the Bagh river and is remarkable as being the only outcrop of sandstone in an otherwise basaltic region. Above the sandstone, however, is superimposed a deep band of claystone, and it is probably to the excessive weight of this band, and to the moisture percolating from it that most of the damage in the caves is due.

The caves, which are nine in number, extend over a frontage of about 750 yards, but are not all contiguous.

CAVE I.

The first, or "Griha," cave calls for no particular notice. The portico, through which it was once approached, has entirely

(1) In the description of the caves which follows, the writer has drawn freely on the accounts of Dr. Impey and Colonel Luard, to whom he gratefully acknowledges his indebtedness. J. M.

vanished and the excavation behind is nothing more than a single chamber, 23 feet by 14 feet, supported on four pillars which are now in a sorry state of dilapidation.

CAVE II.

The second cave (Plate II), known popularly as the *Pandavonki gupha* or Pandava's cave, besides being one of the most elaborate, is also the best preserved of the whole group, though its paintings have long since been obliterated by smoke and bats. It comprises a square monastic hall with cells on three sides, a pillared portico in front, and a stupa chapel in the rear, the overall measurement from front to back being rather more than 150 feet (Plate I). The face of the portico has fallen, and of its six octagonal pillars only the stumps remain (Plate II, *a*). Amid the fallen débris, however, were found fragments of the roof which show that it was adorned in front with a series of *chaitya* medallions inset with tiger masks alternating with lotus flowers. To right and left, in front of the portico, is a niche for an image, sunk in the projecting face of the rock (Plate II, *a*). The one to the left (N.E.) still retains its original but now much defaced sculpture—a Buddha or a Nāga with the usual attendants; in the other is a modern Ganeśa. Access to the hall at the back of the portico is obtained through three doorways, and light and air are admitted through two windows set between them. Both doorways and windows are relieved by a succession of receding reveals, but the only decoration is on the central doorway, where there is a band of carving on the middle lintel and a pilaster supporting it on either side with a small couchant lion at the base. Apart from the portico, entrances and windows on the north-western side, which are indispensable for the admission of air and light, the plan of the monastery is essentially that of the structural monasteries of the time, which consisted of an open court enclosed by ranges of cells, sometimes with a chapel in the middle of one side and invariably with a pillared verandah carried on a raised plinth in front of the cells. The plan was one that must have been as familiar in the domestic architecture of the Orient, as it was in the south of Europe, and was eminently well adapted to the needs of a monastery, since it secured complete privacy to the inmates, and, while protecting them against sun and rain, admitted all the light and air that were required. On the other hand, for rock-cut dwellings it was manifestly inappropriate, inasmuch as the central court was no longer open to the sky, and consequently there was not the same *raison d'être* for the surrounding verandah; nor could sufficient light and air find their way into the cells and chapel. True, the pillars of the verandah served a useful purpose as supports for the roof, and granted that the orthodox plan had to be adhered to, their presence was more or less of a necessity. Given, however, a free hand, the architect might easily have produced a design, which if less conservative, would have been better suited to the requirements of the monks. The twenty pillars in front of the cells as well as the pilasters corresponding to them at the four corners are of varying pattern. All stand on a low square base relieved by a torus moulding, and up to a height of about four feet their shafts are square in section; from that point upwards, however, they are differently treated, some passing through an octagonal to sixteen-sided section, others becoming dodecagonal and twenty-four sided, some with bands of spiral fluting, others of oblique reeding, and others again exhibiting divers other motifs, the character of which will be apparent from the examples reproduced on Plates III and IV. The bracket capitals which surmount them are of a strange type not uncommon in the cave architecture of this period. Seen *en face* they resemble bundles of rods or "fasces" bound together by an ornamental band. The motif, however, is not easy of explanation, for, even if, as seems likely, it was derived from wooden construction, a bracket made on such principles must have been singularly ineffective.

In the centre of the hall is a group of four round columns decorated with fine spiral fluting (Plate V, *a*). These supplementary columns were necessitated by the peculiarly friable nature of the sandstone at Bagh, and are a noteworthy feature of this group of caves. At other sites, such as Ajanta, Ellora, etc., the rock was of better quality and wider spaces than this could be spanned without any intermediate supports.

Including the two to right and left of the front portico, the cells of the monks number twenty. They are small bare chambers averaging less than eight feet in height by a little more in length and breadth with a single lamp niche in each. Connected with the one at the east corner are two unfinished excavations, and behind three others near the north corner are some smaller chambers, at a higher level, which belonged to another and separate cave on the N.E. side, communicating with Cave II by means of a passage. But at the point the rock has now fallen in, and the original plan of this other cave is no longer ascertainable.

The stupa chapel at the back of the hall is approached through a vestibule with a portal in front supported on two columns *in antis*

(Plate I). The walls of the vestibule are adorned with sculptured images in relief, a description of which, from the pen of Prof. J. Ph. Vogel, will be found in another section of this monograph. Here it is enough to state that there is a single standing figure to right and left of the chapel entrance and groups comprising three figures each (a Buddha and two attendants) on the side walls (Plate VI, *a* and *b*). In the middle of the sanctum is a stupa of the customary type carved from the rock and reaching from floor to ceiling (Plates VII, *a* and VIII, *d*).

CAVE III.

The third cave of the series is known locally as the *hathikhana* or elephant stable. Like the second, it seems to have been designed for residential purposes, but its plan is markedly different (Plate VII, *b*), and the fact that the cells have been somewhat more elaborately designed and adorned wth tempera paintings has led to the surmise that they were intended for superior members of the fraternity. Much of the fore-front has fallen, and this part of the plan is to some extent conjectural. It is evident, however, that there must have been a row of chambers on the south-west side corresponding with those on the north-east, and the cave thus consisted of two distinct halls; an outer one supported on eight octagonal columns with a forecourt in front which was flanked, like the hall itself, by a row of cells on either side ; and an inner one, also supported on eight columns but without any connected cells. The chamber set slightly back on the north-east side of the hall and fronted by a pillared vestibule is evidently the most important, and the presence of painted figures of the Buddha on its walls attended by kneeling worshippers suggests that it was a chapel.

In its present time-worn condition this cave strikes the beholder as strangely forbidding and gloomy, but it must have presented a very different appearance when its walls and pillars were enlivened by stucco and paintings. Such fragments of these as have survived are in the same bold and pleasing style as those in the fourth cave to be described anon; and there is also a strikingly bold frieze carved in relief above the front facade. This frieze consists of two bands: in the lower a series of elephants alternating with lions, and in the upper a series of lion masks alternating with *chaitya* windows in which pairs of human busts are inset. The rear hall, be it added, which is connected with the front one by three doorways, has been left in a rough-hewn state, from which it may be inferred that it was a later addition—an inference which is confirmed by some tracings of figures on the parti-wall between the two halls, which were cut through when the doorway to the inner wall was made.

CAVE IV.

The fourth cave, known as the "Rang Mahal" from the paintings which still adorn its walls, was the finest of the group. Between it and Cave III there intervene some 250 feet of rough cliff, but on the further side it is contiguous with Cave V, and in front of these two caves there once stretched a continuous portico more than 220 feet in length and borne on twenty-two pillars (Plate X, *c*). The pillars and much of the overhanging roof of this portico have now fallen, but the pilasters at either end are intact, and on the back wall and roof are many traces of the paintings which formally covered them. In plan and general design Cave IV is very similar to Cave II. There are the same three entrances in front with two square windows intervening between them (Plate X, *b*); the same square hall with pillared verandahs on four sides, ranges of cells on three and a chapel in the rear. The fourth cave, however, is more spacious and in most respects decidedly more elaborate than the second. Thus its central hall is 94 feet across, that is to say eight more than Cave II, and is supported by 38 instead of 24 pillars; while the cells around number eight more than in the other cave. As to the individual cells there is nothing calling for remark except that an extra chamber is added to two of them, *viz.*, to the one on the right hand of the chapel and to another at the south corner. In the latter, the second chamber is sunk below the floor level, access to it being provided in the manner shown in the small section on Plate IX. Compared with the chapel of Cave II, the chapel here is strangely unpretentious, consisting of a single apartment somewhat irregular in plan, with the usual stupa in the middle, but without the pillared portal, vestibule, or sculptured images which distinguish the other.

This unpretentiousness however does not extend to other parts of the cave. The planning of the central hall and the decoration of its various parts, as well as of the doorways and windows opening on to the portico, are much more ambitious. Besides the four supplementary pillars in the middle of the hall—the counterparts of those already noticed in Cave II—there are three[1] highly ornate porches projecting inwards from the middle of the verandah in front of the cells.[2] The columns on which these

(1) The fourth pair of columns shown in the plan on the N.W. side of the hall are, Mr. Garde informs me, a mistake. There was no projecting porch on this side. J.M.

(2) A somewhat similar arrangement is found in the late mediæval monastery at Sarnath.

three porches are sustained are circular in form, furnished with bases and capitals and relieved with finely chiselled fluting or decorative bands (Plate VIII, *a* and XIII). The last mentioned are carved in low relief in a manner specially characteristic of this period,[1] and call to mind the ornamental bands on the lacquered columns of the Mandalay Palace, which are manifestly imitations of beaten metal work. Over the columns and between them and the roof, is a deep entablature, relieved with seated figures of the Buddha in shallow panels, and with *chaitya* windows inset with human masks (Plate VIII, *a*).

The four pillars alluded to above in the middle of the hall, rest on bases cut from the natural rock, and it is evident therefore that they were part and parcel of the original design—not as some have supposed, an afterthought. Owing to some reason or other, however—probably to faults in the rock—the shafts could not be hewn in the same way, and they have been built therefore of small ashlar masonry neatly finished on the face, but somewhat loosely compacted in the core.[2]

Of the 28 pillars of the verandah with their bracket capitals and of the pilasters corresponding to them at the four corners of the hall representative examples are figured in Plates XI, XII and XIV. Both pillars and pilasters are of the same general pattern as those in Cave II, but more diversified in detail, and their bracket capitals are partly painted, partly carved with animals, real or fabulous, in low relief, some with riders some without. The elaborate decoration which distinguishes these pillars extends also to

---

(1) E.g., the pillars at Ajanta figured in Fergusson's *Cave Temples of India*, Pl. XXXVIII, 2 and 3.

(2) It may be noted that the ceiling of this cave was flat, not domical, as suggested by Dr. Impey.

the outer framing of the doorways and windows, the finest of which—the central doorway—is figured in Plate XII, *b*. Across the lintel of this doorway are rows of seated Buddhas and *chaitya* windows inset with heads, while the console at either end takes the form of a standing female figure, her hand resting on the head of a dwarf *(gana)* emerging from the mouth of a *makara*; slender pilasters, with the same motif repeated at their base, support the lintel, and bands of rich floral scrolls and cable moundings complete the framing of the doorway. The consoles, if this term can be properly applied to the projecting ends of the lintels, are specially deserving of notice. In this case they are ornamented in a manner that disconnects them, as it were, from the rest of the lintel. As a rule, however, both in the Gupta and in the preceding Kushan period, the outer band, framing the doorway, whether plain or decorated, is returned round the projections, which it thus serves to emphasise, in precisely the same way as in Græco-Syrian buildings of Western Asia. This treatment of the lintel is such a distinctive feature in itself and so peculiarly characteristic of Græco-Syrian architecture, that there can be little doubt as to its having originated in Western Asia and thence found its way into India. On the other hand, the motif of the woman standing on a *makara* is purely Indian and finds a close analogy in the female figures acting as brackets on the gateways of Sanchi.

CAVE V.

As stated above, the portico fronting Cave IV extended also along the face of Cave V, but whether the two were planned and excavated at one and the same time, is open to question, though the frescoes on the back of the portico seem to indicate that they were contemporary. Cave V (Plates V, X and XV) appears to have served as a refectory or possibly as an oratory. It is a rectangular hall, 95 feet by 44, traversed by two rows of columns, all of the same pattern and singularly plain, their round shafts and cushion capitals being unrelieved by fluting or other devices. Each row stands on a common plinth, which like the architecture above extends from side to side of the hall; and parallel to this plinth at the foot of the walls is a projection of the same height—doubtless intended as a seat.[1] Whatever decoration there was in the hall was restricted to tempera paintings on the walls, columns and ceiling. The same remark also applies to the single doorway and four windows, the triple reveals of which are devoid of carving, but were once stuccoed over and painted like the rest of the portico.

CAVE VI.

Connected with the foregoing by a broad passage and manifestly contemporary with it is a smaller hall above 46 feet square, furnished with five cells—two on the south-western side and three at the rear—intended no doubt for residential purposes (Plate XV, *e*). In the front wall of the cave are a doorway and two windows, which now open out directly on to the valley, but may once have been sheltered by a portico. The octagonal pillars that sustained the roof have fallen, and only slight traces remain of the painted stucco which once bedecked the walls. Indeed, apart from a pair of pilasters at the entrance to the passage leading to Cave V there is practically nothing of a decorative character left in the cave. The design of the two pilasters referred to, however, is peculiar and not without interest. It is a conventionalised derivative of the

(1) Similar seats are provided in the Maharwara Cave at Ellora. Cf. Fergusson, *Cave Temples of India*, p. 373 and Plate LIX.

'pot and foliage' motif, which came into vogue for a short period during the 7th and 8th centuries A.D., and it thus confirms the date for these caves arrived at on other grounds. In this particular instance the motif has been duplicated in order to cover the unusually broad shaft of the pilaster, but in front of Cave IV is another pilaster of more slender proportions on which the motif may be seen in its simpler form.

Of the three remaining Caves (Nos. VII, VIII and IX) there is little to be said. All three have collapsed, and their interiors are choked with masses of rock and débris, which make a complete examination impossible, and which it would hardly be worth while to remove. The stupa and pillars in Cave VII are of the same type that we have already met with in some of the other excavations and the plan also of this cave seems to have been copied from Cave II, though it has none of the sculptured decorations which beautify the latter.

In concluding these remarks on the architecture of the Bagh Caves, I cannot refrain from adding a few words about the technique and general character of the paintings, which, whatever their iconographic significance, constitute an integral and inseparable part of the scheme of decoration. At Bagh, as at Ajanta, the paintings are done in *tempera*, not, as has often been stated, in *fresco*, and the processes and colours employed at both places seem to have been the same. At Bagh, however, less care has been taken over the preparation of the first rough coat (rinfazzo). As at Ajanta, this coat is made of the local ferruginous earth compounded with gravel, lime and the fibres of jute and hemp. The work, however, has been done in a somewhat slipshod manner, and as a consequence, the rinfazzo is less tenacious than at Ajanta—a defect that has contributed in no small measure to the deterioration of the paintings. On the other hand, as far as their artistry is concerned, there is little to choose between the pictures of Bagh and Ajanta. Both exhibit the same broad handling of their subjects, the same poetry of motion, the same wonderful diversity in the poses of their figures, the same feeling for colour and the same strong yet subtle line-work. In both, decorative beauty is the key-note to which all else is attuned, and both are as free from realism as they are from stereotype convention. The artists, to be sure, have portrayed their subjects direct from life—of that there can be no shadow of doubt, but however fresh and vital the portrayal may be, it never misses that quality of abstraction which is indispensable to mural decoration, as it is, indeed, to all truly great painting. True, there is nothing left at Bagh to equal some of the surpassingly majestic figures, such as the famous Bodhisattva, at Ajanta; but in one respect at any rate the paintings of Bagh have an advantage over those of Ajanta. For whereas at Ajanta most of the paintings appear to have been done piecemeal—according, it may be presumed, as benefactions were made by successive donors—at Bagh they give the impression of having been conceived and executed at one and the same time, or at any rate in conformity with a single well-thought-out scheme. There is nothing in Ajanta so striking, from a purely decorative point of view, as the splendidly bold frieze of swags in Caves IV and V, which call to mind the magnificent bands of ornament on the contemporary Dhamekh Stupa at Sarnath; nor is there anything at Ajanta more masterly in conception and composition than the groups illustrated in Plate XVI. The pity is that the full effect of these paintings cannot be brought out in the small illustrations of a monograph such as this. To be adequately appreciated they must be seen to their full scale and in the architectural setting for which they were designed.

MISCELLANEOUS NOTES ON BAGH CAVES

By M. B. GARDE, B.A.,

Superintendent of Archæology, Gwalior State.

GENERAL

The caves are excavated in a sandstone hill in the Vindhyan range on the left bank of a small tributary of the Narmada—the river Wagh or Bagh—from which the caves, as also the nearest town, take their names. The tract of country for miles around is hilly and covered with low jungle. Bagh is a small town with a population of 2,000 situated at 22° 22' North and 74° 48' East. Being the head-quarters of a sub Tehsil in the Amjhera District of Gwalior State, there is a Niab Tehsildar's office, a police station, a village school, a dispensary and a state post office, the nearest telegraph office, however, being at Kukshi, 12 miles away.

ANTIQUARIAN REMAINS

About a quarter of a mile to the South West of the town, on a low hill, vestiges of early habitation are seen in the shape of brick foundations. These are traditionally referred to Mordhaj or Mayuradhvaja, a mythical king. But the earliest antiquities to which a date can be assigned—some stray stone sculptures representing the Seven Mothers which have been found in the neighbourhood of Bagh—can only be taken back to the 5th or 6th century A.D. Half-a-mile to the East of the town on the bank of the Bagh river are mere traces of a group of rock-cut caves distinct from those which form the subject of the present monograph. Close by stands an 11th century temple of Siva, locally known as Mahakalesvara. It had a brick *sikhara* which has now fallen away, but the basement walls, which are of stone, decorated on the exterior with bold cornices and bands of geometrical designs, are still in good preservation. Quite recently a stone image of Brahman with an inscription dated in V. S. 1210 and mentioning Yasodhavala, a Paramara Chief, has been found in the town. On the north of the town and overlooking it, is a small fort in the Muhammadan style, now in ruins, but a necessity for a place of any importance in the turbulent times of the 17th and 18th centuries. The Baghesvari Temple is a modern reconstruction of little antiquarian interest.

FOR VISITORS

Bagh is an out-of-the-way place, no doubt. But the dangers and difficulties of the journey have often been exaggerated. A trip to Bagh was never (in modern times) so unsafe and beset with dangers as some would have us believe, not to speak of the vast improvement in the facilities of communications that has taken place in recent years.

Bagh caves are 90 miles by road from the nearest Railway Station, Mhow, on the Rajputana Malwa section of the B. B. & C.

I. Railway. Mhow is a British Military Cantonment with a Travellers' Bungalow and a Hotel under European management. A good metalled road from Mhow to the town of Bagh (a distance of some 87 miles), passes through Dhar—the capital of a Maratha State—and Sardarpur, once a British Military Cantonment, but now the headquarters of the Amjhera District of Gwalior State. There are Travellers' Bungalows at convenient stages all along this road including a small but commodious Bungalow near Bagh town. (Travellers have to make their own arrangement for food, no European provisions being available at Bagh).

The caves are between two and three miles from the Bagh Bungalow, and this distance is at present covered for the most part by a fair-weather track, which though motorable for nearly eight months in the year is on the whole rather troublesome, as it crosses the dry but sandy bed of the Bagh river more than once. It is now proposed to extend the metalled road right up to the caves, and to build a small rest house near the caves for the convenience of such visitors as would like to stay there over-night.

Taxi cars are easily available at Mhow, and the journey each way can be made comfortably in half-a-day (6 hours). The best plan for a visitor would be to engage a car for two days, to start from Mhow after breakfast, to rest for the night at the Bagh Bungalow, or at the rest house near the caves, to see the caves the following morning and to make the return journey in the afternoon.

CHRONOLOGY OF THE CAVES

There is not a single inscription on the caves to help us to unravel the tale of so important a monument. The same reason, namely—the bad quality of rock—which accounts for the paucity of sculpture ornament is also responsible for the absence of inscriptions on these caves. And just as the want of decorative carving was compensated for by the sister art of painting, so there is ground to believe that painted records served the purpose of inscriptions. Unfortunately these have perished altogether leaving a solitary *ka* painted in Indian red—obviously the remnant of a label—which is still seen under the scene of the procession of horsemen on the back wall of the portico of caves Nos. 4 and 5. On palæographical grounds this *ka* is referable to the 6th or 7th century, and that this is roughly the age of the caves is confirmed by their architecture, sculpture and, above all, paintings. On the evidence of these three the caves may safely be classed with some of the late but not the latest *Viharas* at Ajanta. Among themselves, cave No. 1, with its simple four-pillared hall is probably the earliest. Caves Nos. 2 and 3 which come next, with their clumsy pillars are perhaps to be ranked with the 20 pillared cave No. 12, at Ajanta. Cave No. 4 may be contemporary with the cave bearing the same number at Ajanta, although the paintings on the former are allied to those on caves Nos. 16 and 17 at Ajanta. Caves Nos. 4, 5 and 6, connected as they are either externally through the portico as caves Nos. 4 and 5, or internally through a passage as caves Nos. 5 and 6 would appear to be contemporary and chronologically the last of the surviving caves in this group. The caves are manifestly the work of Mahayana Buddhists, though there is one anomaly, namely, that the principal object of worship is here the pure and simple Dagoba and not the figure of the Buddha.

LITERATURE

These caves were discovered in modern times, or at any rate first described to the world of antiquarians by Lieutenant Dangerfield, of the Bombay Military Establishment, as early as 1818 (*Transactions of the Literary Society of Bombay*, Volume II, pp. 206-214). The Lieutenant was by no means a student of Buddhism or Indian architecture. Besides he took notes in one day's hurried visit, and had in those days no aid of photography for the verification of his notes. His article therefore reads rather crude, and as he had only the notions of his ignorant guides to go by he was unable to divine the correct nature of the excavations (*e.g.* he calls the cells of the monks *dookans* or shops). This was for the first time done by Mr. W. Erskine in a note which he appended to the Lieutenant's paper. The first scholar who, however, approached the subject with some knowledge of Buddhism, its history and architecture, was Dr. E. Impey, who contributed a lengthy and learned paper on the caves, to the *Journal of the Bombay Branch of the Royal Asiatic Society* (Volume V, pp. 543-73). Herein he described the details of their architecture and painting with minuteness, and on the whole with great precision, although, as was excusable in those days, some misconceptions have crept in this by far the fullest account of the caves so far published (*e.g.* his hypothesis of a domical ceiling and a second *Dagoba* in the hall of cave No. 4). Colonel C. E. Luard(1) to whom belongs the credit of having roused the necessary interest for the publication of this monograph, visited the caves some time in 1907 or 1908,

(1) It was at his instance that the accompanying architectural drawings published now for the first time were prepared by Mr. Asgar Ali Khan, of the Gwalior Public Works Department. Gwalior had not yet had its own Archæological Department. The caves were then in a neglected condition, full of debris, and accurate measurements of certain parts of the caves were impracticable. The caves are now freed from debris and the drawings verified and corrected where necessary by the Gwalior Archæological Department.

while he was in charge of the compilation of Central India Gazetteers, and in 1910 published in the *Indian Antiquary* a paper which (as he has acknowledged) is an abridged summary of Dr. Impey's account improved upon in the light of his own personal information, and, what is more important, accompanied by a good many photographic illustrations. To this may be added Mr. A. K. Haldar's paper in the *Burlington Magazine* (October 1923), and Mr. M. C. Dey's book "My pilgrimage to Ajanta and Bagh." (1925)

THE WORK OF THE GWALIOR ARCHÆOLOGICAL DEPARTMENT

On the creation of the Archæological Department in Gwalior the caves began to receive the attention they deserved, and active measures were devised to maintain them as well as possible. Owing to the bad quality of the rock many of the pillars and parts of walls and roofs had crumbled down and most of the caves had been choked up with an enormous mass of their own debris. Many of the door and window openings were blocked up, which made the entry even of light and air into the interior difficult. All the debris has now been cleared off and arranged into a sort of platform or landing place in front of the caves making them easy of access. Further, the work of repairing decayed walls, underpinning decayed pillars and building up masonry supports to prop up large overhanging spans of ceiling where original monolithic pillars have either partially or wholly decayed or disappeared, is in progress. But the most useful work of the Department has been with regard to the copying and preservation of the valuable paintings which have partially survived, but which are gradually disappearing. For this purpose paid services of some of the best artists available in the country, namely: Messrs. Nanda Lal Bose, Asit Kumar Haldar and Surendra Nath Kar, of Calcutta; Messrs. A. B. Bhonsle and B. A. Apte, of Bombay; and Messrs. M. S. Bhand and V. B. Jagtap, of Gwalior, were secured.

The illustrations of paintings reproduced in this monograph are prepared from these copies which are now exhibited in the Archæological Museum at Gwalior, and duplicates[1] from these in the British Museum, London. The original paintings exist on the back wall of the common portico of caves Nos. 4 and 5. The roof of the portico having given way the paintings are exposed to weather, perhaps for centuries. A suitable shed or cover to protect them *in situ* will be constructed shortly.

(1) The subjoined table specifies the work of individual artists:

Plate	Subject in Colours	Copying Artist	Plate	Subject in Colours	Copying Artist
A	The First Scene	Mr. S. N. Kar	F	The Fifth Scene	Mr. B. A. Apte
B	The Second Scene	Mr. B. A. Apte	G	The Sixth Scene	Messrs. Bhonsle & Apte
C	The Third Scene	Mr. M. S. Bhand	H	The Sixth Scene (detail)	Mr. A. K. Haldar
D	The Fourth Scene (left)	Mr. N. L. Bose	I	The Sixth Scene (detail)	Mr. V. B. Jagtap
E	The Fourth Scene (right)	Mr. A. B. Bhonsle			

Outlines in monocolour: Messrs. Bose, Haldar, Kar and Apte

THE SCULPTURES AND PAINTINGS.

ICONOGRAPHICAL DESCRIPTION.

By DR. J. PH. VOGEL.

I Sculptures.

a. Buddhas and Bodhisattvas.

The evolution of the Buddhist Caves of India from the very simple prototypes of the pre-Christian age to the complicated and ornate examples of the Gupta epoch has been set forth by Fergusson and other authors and need not be repeated. The great change in architecture (if we may use this term) and ornamentation exhibited by the later caves is in a large measure due to an all important fact in the history of Buddhist religion and art—the creation of the Buddha image. Whereas in the early caves the central cult object is the *stūpa* or relic monument, we find that ancient emblem now gradually replaced by the effigy of the Master. In the decoration, too, the image of the Buddha becomes more and more prominent, until at last we find that monotonous and senseless repetition of Buddha figures which is so characteristic of later Buddhist art.

The creation of the Buddha image affected not only the *chaitya* cave (i.e. the shrine in which the *chaitya* or *stūpa* was the object of worship) but also the *vihāra* which in its origin was exclusively intended for the accommodation of the *bhikshus*. The Caves of Bagh, as has been pointed out above, belong to the latter class. After the image of the Buddha had come into existence, it was felt that his effigy ought to occupy the place of honour in the central cell opposite the entrance, in the same manner as during his life time the Master was believed to have occupied a special cell, the *gandhakuṭī*, in the famous Jetavana Convent near Śrāvastī. In the course of time the Buddha cell develops into a shrine or chapel.

In this respect the Nāsik Caves are particularly instructive. They belong, as is well known, to the category of early caves and may be assigned to the reign of the satrap Nahapāna (*c.* 100 A.D.) whose son-in-law Ushavadāta is mentioned in inscriptions. In the large *vihāra*, No. 3, the centre of the back-wall of the big hall is carved with a *stūpa* between the usual adoring figures. A similar bas-relief in exactly the same position opposite the entrance must once have existed in *vihāra* No. 8 (now 10), but here it has been hewn into an ugly figure of Bhairava. We may safely assume that in both cases the *chaitya* which was the first to draw the eye of anyone entering the cave, was meant to be an object of worship. Now it is not a little curious that in the *vihāra*, No. 20, which is contemporaneous with the other caves of the group, the bas-relief in question has been replaced by a chapel which consists of a vestibule or anteroom and a sanctum, the latter containing a Buddha seated between two Bodhisattvas. The two pillars and two pilasters of the anteroom have capitals in the shape of vases with overhanging foliage, entirely different in style from the columns of the verandah which are distinguished by bell-shaped capitals with recumbent animals. It is evident that the chapel must be a later addition of the Gupta period when pillars of the pot-and-foliage type are known to have come into vogue.

The *vihāra* Caves of Ajaṇṭā belonging to the Gupta epoch are regularly provided with such a chapel, usually consisting of a vestibule and a sanctum enshrining a large rock-cut image of the Buddha seated in the preaching attitude between two Bodhisattvas standing.

The monastic Caves of Bagh represent a transitional stage: the cave No. 2 is indeed provided with a chapel, but the sanctuary contains the ancient object of worship in the form of a rock-cut *chaitya* (Plate VII a). This *chaitya* has a hemispherical dome supporting a *harmikā* and parasol, and rests on a cylindrical drum, decorated with a modillion cornice, which in its turn is placed on an octagonal plinth with bold mouldings.

Whereas, therefore, the *chaitya* still retains the place of honour as chief object of worship, a number of rock-cut figures of Buddhas and Bodhisattvas are arrayed along the walls of the vestibule. Both the side walls are decorated with a group of three standing statues of more than life-size, evidently in each case a Buddha between two Bodhisattvas, the central figure exceeding the latter in height. As the two groups are very similar, it will suffice to describe only that on the right hand side which excels both by its preservation and artistic merit (Plate VI, *a*). The Buddha (height 10 ft. 4 ins.) in the centre is shown standing on a conventional lotus-flower with his right arm stretched down, the palm of the hand open in the attitude which in Buddhist iconography is known as the gift-bestowing gesture (Skt. *varadamudrā*). The left hand holds the hem of the garment in front of the shoulder, a feature met with both in the art of Gandhāra and in that of Mathurā,(1) where, however, the right hand is invariably raised in the attitude of protection (Skt. *abhayamudrā*). In later Buddhist art, beginning from the Gupta period, the raised left hand is often combined with the *varadamudrā* of the right hand, as is the case at Bagh.

The Buddha is clad in an ample robe which leaves the right shoulder bare, the drapery being indicated by schematic folds. The outline of the body is clearly indicated in the manner of the Gupta period. The head has the usual little curls and the protuberance of the skull (Skt. *ushṇīsha*) which belong to the thirty-two signs of the *mahāpurusha*.(2) The *ūrṇā* between the eye-brows which is another mark of the Bodhi is absent, but possibly it was indicated in paint. For there can be little doubt that these images were once covered with a thin layer of plaster, as is still found on some images at Ajaṇṭā, and that this plaster was painted. At Bagh, too, traces of *chunam* subsist.

Of the two attendants the one (height 9 ft.) to the right of the Buddha is shown standing on a lotus with his left leg slightly advanced. In his right hand he holds the handle of a chowrie or fly-whisk in such a manner that the bushy part hangs over his right shoulder. His left hand rests on the knot formed by the upper garment which is wrapped round his loins in a manner not unusual in images of the Kushāṇa and Gupta periods. The lower

(1) A. Foucher, *L'art gréco-bouddhique du Gandhāra* Vol. II., Figs. 583-4 and 588. *Catalogue of the Archæological Museum at Mathurā*, Pl. XVa.

(2) Grünwedel and Burgess, *Buddhist Art in India*, p. 161.

garment is indicated by the presence of a jewelled girdle meant to keep it up. The figure wears the ornaments usually found on Bodhisattva images—a crown and ear-rings, a double necklace, bracelets round the wrists and a triple thread probably meant for a *janev* or Brahmanical cord. The left hand is slightly damaged; otherwise the image is well preserved.

The other satellite (height 8 ft. 3 ins.), standing on a lotus to the left of the Buddha, wears no crown but has long curly locks with a top-knot. He, too, has ornaments consisting of ear-rings, a double necklace, and bracelets round the upper arms and the wrists. In his right hand he holds a bunch of lotus-buds, whilst his left is applied to the knot formed by the upper garment which likewise is slung round his waist. The left hand is slightly injured.

The group occupying the opposite or northern wall (Plate VI, *b*) is somewhat smaller in size, the Buddha measuring 9 ft. 6 ins., and the two attendants nearly 7 ft. in height. The attitude and attributes are the same as in the group first described. The figure to the left of the Buddha is considerably injured in consequence of a crack which runs right through the body from the left shoulder to the right hip. The top of the head and the face are also damaged.

It is well known that groups of a Buddha flanked by two Bodhisattvas are very frequent in Buddhist art. In the numerous examples belonging to the medieval period the two satellites of the Buddha are usually Avalokiteśvara and Maitreya clearly distinguished, the one by a lotus-flower whence his epithet Padmapāṇi, and the other by a *nāgapushpa*(1) held in each case in the left hand. More-

(1) This flower must be identical with the *champaka* (Michelia Champaka). Cf. A. Foucher, *Étude sur l'iconographie bouddhique de l'Inde* (1900), p. 113 and (1905), p. 49.

over, Avalokiteśvara wears a figurine of Amitābha, the Buddha of Boundless Light, inserted in his diadem, whereas Maitreya has a *mukuṭa* decorated with a miniature *stūpa* in front.

It will be seen that in the case of the two groups described above there are no such distinctive marks which might enable us to identify the two attending personages. It is true that in either case the figure to the Buddha's left carries a bunch of lotus-buds, but this would hardly justify us in identifying him with Avalokita, as the lotus characterising this Bodhisattva in later Buddhist art is invariably held in the left hand. All we can say is that evidently it was the intention of the sculptor to differentiate the two attending figures, as in both groups the one to the right of the Buddha holds a chowrie and wears a crown, whereas the other attendant holds lotus-flowers and has long locks with a top-knot but no crown. It is noteworthy that in Gandhāran sculpture too, where we find the earliest examples of such triads, there is not only the same tendency towards differentiation but the distinctive mark is also the head-dress. This is a point of some interest, although in other respects the two groups under discussion show little connection with their Gandhāran prototypes, in which the central Buddha figure is always seated in the attitude of expounding the law (Skt. *dharmachakramudrā*).

The doorway giving access to the inner shrine is flanked by two stately statues more rigid than those decorating the side walls of the anteroom. They are placed in arched niches. The one on the left hand (Plate VIII, *b*) measures 8 ft. 3 ins. in height and is distinguished by a very lofty and elaborate *jaṭāmukuṭa* containing a miniature Buddha figure seated in the *abhayamudrā*. On both sides of this central ornament there are two miniature animals, perhaps meant for lions, which seem to hold a wreath. On both sides of the head there is a radiating nimbus-like ornament which appears to be part of the head-dress.(1) In this connection it may be pointed out that none of the images found at Bagh except the supposed Yaksha described beneath is provided with a nimbus.

The figure under discussion wears rich ornaments—a triple necklace consisting of two strings of pearls or beads with a breast ornament between, a threefold cord in the manner of a *janev*, fastened on the left side of the breast by means of a large clasp, bracelets on the upper arms and wrists and a jewelled girdle by which the lower garment (*dhotī*) is fastened round the waist. This garment is indicated not only by means of schematic folds visible on the legs of the statue but also in the form of drapery carved on both sides. The central portion hanging down between the legs recalls the Bodhisattva images of the Kushāṇa period. The upper portion of the body above the girdle is uncovered. The right hand is broken, and any emblem which it may once have held is lost. The left hand is applied to the thigh. The image stands on a conventional lotus which is badly carved and may be due to an afterthought.

The corresponding figure (Plate VIII, *c*) on the right hand side of the entrance to the sanctum is of nearly the same size (height 8 ft. 9 ins.) and stands also on a lotus, but in its general appearance

(1) Dr. Impey, op. cit. p. 552, calls it "an open disk or glory," but more probably it is part of the head-dress. The same arrangement is found in two Bodhisattva images from Sānchi, preserved in the local museum. Cf. *Catalogue, of the Museum of Archæology at Sanchi, Bhopal State*, Calcutta, 1922, p. 33, Nos. A 100 and 101.

it is much plainer than the image first described. It is devoid of ornaments. The matted hair is tied up on the top of the head so as to form a high head-dress in which a Buddha figurine seated in *abhayamudrā* is inserted between two flower-rosettes.(1) The lower half of the body down to the ankles, is clad in a *dhotī* which is fastened round the waist by means of a simple waist-band. The folds are marked in parallel horizontal lines across the legs.

The right arm is stretched downwards. The right hand is broken, but was evidently in the gift-bestowing gesture and may have held a rosary (Skt. *akshamālā*). The left hand clasps the short spout of a water-flask (Skt. *kamaṇḍalu*), half of which is broken.

Here, as elsewhere, the ancient sanctuaries of a banished religion attract Hindu worshippers who do not hesitate to recognise in the Buddhist images the effigies of the principal heroes and heroines of the *Mahābhārata*. The two guardians of the holy entrance they readily identify with Dharmarāja, *i.e.* Yudhishṭhira, the eldest of the five Pāṇḍavas, and with his great cousin and counsellor, the divine Kṛishṇa. The triad carved on the right hand wall they declare to represent Kuntī with her two remaining sons Bhīma and Arjuna, whilst the corresponding group on the left is believed to portray the twins Nakula and Sahadeva together with Draupadī, the common spouse of the five brothers. The Buddha, it will be noticed, is made to masquerade in either case for a female personage of the Great Epic.

It is far from easy to decide on the real meaning of the two statues described above. Dr. Burgess,(2) in reproducing the right

(1) It is not clear what Dr. Impey, op. cit. p. 552, means by the "lambent flame of sanctity" expanded behind the head of this figure.

(2) Grünwedel and Burgess, *Buddhist Art in India*, p. 193, fig. 141. The interpretation is evidently due to Dr. Burgess, as the passage in which it occurs is not found in the German original.

hand figure, asserts that the presence of the Buddha figurine in the head-dress " precludes doubt that the representation is that of Avalokiteśvara." If, however, we take into consideration that both doorkeepers have such a miniature Buddha inserted in their head-dress and that, moreover, in either case this Buddha is represented in the *abhayamudrā* and not in the *dhyānamudrā* required for Avalokita's spiritual father Amitābha, it will be admitted that there exists, indeed, good reason to doubt the proposed identification.

Here again it is obvious that the artist who fashioned these two statues or the pious donor who guided his hand, had the intention to make a clear distinction between them. In other words, they were not meant for a pair of anonymous satellites like the chowrie-carriers who sometimes attend the Buddhas of Mathurā during the Kushāṇa period. They must represent two distinct personages of the Buddhist Pantheon. Now it is a point of interest that in each of the three pairs of Bodhisattvas found at Bagh the one to the proper left is much plainer in appearance than his companion on the proper right. The same difference is noticeable in several sculptures of the Gupta period found at Sārnāth, although the place assigned to the two attendants at the side of the Buddha is here reversed. The attendants have usually the function of chowrie-bearers, as is also the case at Mathurā and Ajaṇṭā, but in some specimens from Sārnāth the one in plain dress who stands to the right of the Buddha holds an *akshamālā*, a *kamaṇḍalu* and an *ajina*, whereas the one to the Buddha's left holds the *padma* in his left hand.[1] In these examples the former figure in the attire of a Brahmachārin may be safely identified as Maitreya, the future

(1) Cf. D. R. Sahni, *Catalogue of the Museum of Archæology at Sārnāth*, pp. 72f., No. B (*b*) 186, and p. 105, No. B (*c*) 110.

Buddha, who is predestined to be born in a Brahmanical family. The other is characterised by his lotus-flower as Avalokiteśvara or Padmapāṇi.

On the strength of the evidence supplied by the Sārnāth sculptures there is some reason to assume that at Bagh too the Bodhisattva in simple attire represents Maitreya, and that the more ornate figure to the Buddha's right is Avalokiteśvara.

It has been conjectured that the triads of a Buddha between two Bodhisattvas which we are discussing, are derived from similar groups in which Buddha is placed between the Brahmanical gods Brahmā and Śakra. Such groups are very common in the Graeco-Buddhist school of Gandhāra. The hypothesis referred to is to a certain extent confirmed by the above observations. It is indeed perfectly plausible that the figure of Brahmā has developed into the priestly personage in whom we have recognized Maitreya, and that Śakra the ancient chief of the Devas, finally became the princely figure known among the Buddhists as Avalokiteśvara.

b. Minor Deities.

M. Foucher[1] has drawn attention to the interesting fact that at Ajaṇṭā we find the worship of Buddha associated with the cult of lower divinities which might be more aptly described as spirits than as gods. In other ancient Buddhist sites all over India there is plenty of evidence to the same effect, and we may add that the phenomenon is also observable in the living Buddhism of Burma. The cult of Yakshas, Nāgas, and other godlings does not pertain to any particular creed, but is common to Brahmanism, Buddhism,

(1) *Rapport préliminaire sur l'interprétation des peintures et sculptures d'Ajanta* [1920], p. 45.

and Jainism. Nor is it difficult to account for the great popularity which from earliest times those minor deities enjoyed and still enjoy among broad masses of the rural and urban population of India. Deities of this type are, no doubt, deemed to be more accessible and open to supplication than the supreme divinities of the Brahmanical and Buddhist Pantheons. Besides, the Yakshas and Nāgas are believed to minister unto the immediate wants of ordinary humanity by granting wealth, abundant rain for the crops, and offspring.

Among the sculptures of Ajaṇṭā the Yakshas and Nāgas are well represented. We may quote first of all the graceful group of a Nāgarāja with his queen and a female attendant, which is placed on the left side of the court in front of the *chaitya* hall, No. 19. From the *vihāra*, No. 16, some steps lead down to a small rock-cut chapel in which a fine Nāga figure, unfortunately much damaged, with high diadem is seated in *lalitāsana* pose on the coils of a serpent whose polycephalous hood forms a canopy over his head. At the right end of the verandah of the *vihāra* Cave No. 1 there is a fine panel showing a five-hooded Nāga with attendants and on the opposite or left end a similar panel portrays the Yakshī Hārītī seated with a child in her lap. Nāgas are also found as doorkeepers on both sides of the entrance to several of the Ajaṇṭā Caves.

The Yaksharājas which are characterised by their corpulence as givers of wealth and prosperity, not only occupy a prominent position on the façade of the *chaitya* hall, No. 19, on both sides of the big horse-shoe arched window,(1) but they often receive the distinction of special chapels. In the *vihāra* Cave, No. 2, of Ajaṇṭā

(1) Fergusson, *History of Indian and Eastern Architecture*, 2nd ed. revised by Burgess, vol. I., p. 152, fig. 74.

they even occupy the two subsidiary shrines on both sides of the sanctuary in which the Buddha image is enshrined. The left hand chapel contains the figures of two Yaksharājas, seated side by side, whilst the corresponding shrine on the right shows a group of a male and female Yaksha with their numerous offspring in which we recognise Pāñchika, the general, and his consort Hārītī. Similar groups in which Fergusson saw a "Buddhist Holy Family," are also found at Ellora. Painted figures of Yakshas must once have adorned the left end of the verandah of the *vihāra* Cave, No. 17, of Ajaṇṭā. The figures themselves have almost entirely vanished, but an inscription is still extant recording the name of one of them to be Maṇibhadra.

The Bagh Caves, too, afford evidence of that curious mixture of Buddhism with more primitive cults to which reference has been made above. Unfortunately the figures of Yakshas and Nāgas found here, owing to their exposed position in front of the caves, have suffered such severe damage as to be now well-nigh irrecognisable. We will attempt to describe what is left.

At the northern end of the verandah of Cave No. 2 there is an exterior recess which contains a group of figures carved on the back wall (Plate I). The surface of the stone has deteriorated to such an extent that it is impossible to identify them with certainty. If we may judge from what we find at Ajaṇṭā, it seems most likely that the central figure of the group represents a demi-god, either a Yaksha or a Nāga. On account of its slim waist the figure in all probability is not a Yaksha, who as a rule is corpulent, but a Nāga. In fact, faint traces of the usual cobra-hood seem still to subsist. The central figure at any rate appears to represent a male deity seated in the *lalitāsana* pose on a kind of bench. On both sides an attendant, probably female, much smaller in size is shown standing, but whether these satellites held chowries or any other objects it is now impossible to decide.[1]

The carved panel is enclosed between two pilasters, one of which in its capital clearly shows the familiar device of the flower-vase with overhanging foliage. Beneath are carvings indicating a *siṃhāsana* adorned with four lions. The two in the middle are shown facing, only the head, forequarter and fore-paws being shown. Those at the two extremities are of the usual type : they are turned outward, apparently with one forepaw raised. To the proper left side of this *siṃhāsana* there projects a *makara* head, such as is commonly used to decorate the back of a throne; the corresponding *makara* on the proper right is absent. Over the shrine here described the surface of the rock retains some remnants of carving. A horse-shoe arch surmounted by two flying celestials carrying a garland can still be made out.

In front of the opposite end of the verandah there is a similar shrine. It must contain an ancient image carved in relief, but this is now concealed under a mud idol of a seated Gaṇeśa. In the course of worship the elephant-headed god is freely besmeared with redlead (Hindī *sindūr*) and a little earthenware lamp (*diyā*) may be seen burning in the corner. The ancient carvings are still visible beneath this modern production: they consist of drapery hanging down from lion's heads which alternate with a kind of rosettes. On the rock above there are traces of a decoration similar to that found over the corresponding shrine at the northern

---

(1) Dr. Impey, op. cit. p. 548, speaks of "traces of chowree bearers."

end of the verandah. Here, too, we notice an arch, but of the two garland-carriers only one is partly preserved.

At the side of the large *vihāra* Cave, No. 4, to the north-east, there is a deep niche (height 14 ft. 9 ins.), facing the north-west, which enshrines a seated figure (Plate X b). On account of its colossal size, it can be discerned from a considerable distance by persons approaching the caves. Unfortunately, owing to the process of disintegration to which the surface of the stone has been subject, large portions of this image have fallen away. Both the head and the entire lower half of the body with the exception of the left leg are lost. The right arm, too, is worn away. The statue represents a very corpulent personage with thick rounded limbs and much abdominal development. The left foot is placed on the ground; the right leg which is entirely gone, was probably drawn up in the pose known as *lalitāsana*. The left hand rests on the thigh. The figure wears various ornaments. There are traces of heavy ear-pendants and on the left shoulder we notice a kind of riband. On the breast there are remnants of an elaborate necklace and the upper part of both arms is adorned with a jewelled bracelet, that on the proper right being only partly preserved.

The circular halo which is still traceable round the head marks the divine nature of the personage represented. It is, however, impossible to make out any distinctive emblems which would enable us to identify him. At the side of the left knee the stone shows a projection which may be the remnant of a money bag but which equally well may have been drapery such as subsists at the side of the leg. The position and general appearance of the sculpture suggest a Yaksharāja, such as are also found at Ajaṇṭā and Ellora, but owing to its very fragmentary state, a more precise identification of this image is out of the question.

On both sides of the shoulders a well-carved *makara* head projects sideways. The one to the proper left is well preserved, only part of the upper jaw with the curled-up proboscis being missing. These *makara* heads are regularly employed to decorate the projecting ends of the cross-beam belonging to the back of the throne on which the deity is seated. The earliest examples of this decorative motif occur in the sculptures of Amarāvatī. Henceforward it is regularly found not only in the later art of India both Brahmanical and Buddhist, but also in the Buddhist art of Java.

The surface of the rock above the image niche shows some carvings. Right over the image we notice a *stūpa* with two parasols and two flying figures enclosed between pilasters. Nearer the *vihāra* two shrines are carved in the rock. On the left hand side, too, there are remnants of a similar relief, but a large layer of the rock has collapsed so that the lower half of these carvings has disappeared.

At the north-east end of the verandah belonging to the large *vihāra* Cave, No. 4, there is a little rock-cut Nāga shrine (Plate Xb), the outer wall of which on the side towards the valley has entirely gone. On the side towards the *vihāra* an ornamental pilaster with bracket capital is still preserved. The panel (width 5 ft. 5 ins., height 5 ft. 1 in.) forming the back of this little shrine contains two rock-cut figures which, although considerably injured owing to disintegration, still admit of identification. Of these two figures the one to the proper right is a male, the other apparently a female, both being seated side by side on a bench which is void of all decoration. The male personage sits in the *lalitāsana* or easy posture with his right foot placed on the ground and his left leg drawn up. A seven-fold cobra-hood[1] which is fairly well preserved characterises him as a Nāgarāja. Both his hands are placed on his thighs; it is impossible to say whether they once held any emblem. If they did so, all trace thereof has disappeared.

His female companion seated at his side can hardly be anything else but the consort of the Nāgarāja, although the single serpent-crest which usually distinguishes the Nāgī is no longer traceable. Both her feet rest on the ground. Her right hand was probably raised to the height of the shoulder, the open palm turned to front, in the attitude called *abhayamudrā* which indicates the imparting of security or protection. Her left hand rests on her left knee.

The ledge over the panel here described is fashioned in the manner of a curvilinear roof decorated in the centre with a horse-shoe arch of very small size and at both sides with a vase or treasure pot. The rock supplying the wall of the Nāga chapel is painted inside with rows of miniature Buddhas seated cross-legged, apparently five in each row.[2]

The surface of the rock immediately above the Nāga chapel is carved in the shape of a rectangular panel enclosed between two pilasters with shafts polygonal in section and capitals of the pot-and-foliage type. The panel contains a horse-shoe arch, the interior carvings of which have almost entirely disappeared. But

(1) This distinctive is also noted by Dr. Impey, op. cit. p. 555.

(2) Dr. Impey, op. cit. p. 555, speaks of "eight rows of diminutive Buddhas, within pointed canopies."

from the little that remains it may be safely concluded that inside the arch there was a figure of the Buddha preaching his first sermon, a subject frequently met with at Kārlī and Ajaṇṭā. Not only the top of the Buddha's head with the well-known little curls is preserved and two chowries which must have belonged to attendants standing to his right and left, but also the emblem of the wheel between the two antelopes is visible beneath. The two spandrels on both sides of the arch are each occupied by a flying figure, perhaps a Gandharva, carrying a garland.

We now wish to draw attention to the two female figures (Plate XIIb) each standing on a *makara* or conventional crocodile, which decorate the central doorway of the *vihāra* Cave, No. 4, and which are also to be reckoned among the minor deities. Both these figures are placed under a tree with overhanging foliage; the left-hand tree appears to be a mango, the other is perhaps a custard-apple (Hindī *sītāphal).* In each case the right hand of the goddess is raised and holds a branch of the tree, whilst her left hand rests on the head of an attendant of miniature size who may be either a child or a dwarf. The attendant to the proper left is a male, the one to the proper right a female.

Similar figures are regularly found in exactly the same position on both sides of the doorway not only in the Buddhist caves of Ajaṇṭā but also in the Brahmanical temples of the Gupta period. The earliest examples known are the rock-cut shrines of Udayagiri (Gwalior State), of which the so-called "Cave of Chandragupta" bears an inscription dated in the Gupta year 82, corresponding to A.D. 401. Now it has been recognized long ago that there must be a close connection between the female figures under discussion and the images of Gaṅgā and Yamunā which are regularly found on both sides of the doorway of the medieval temples of India. It would, however, be rash to conclude, as has been done by some writers, that the figures at Ajaṇṭā and Bagh must have the same meaning. These figures, as has been pointed out in the course of our description, are both placed on a crocodile, whereas in the case of the two river-goddesses the *vāhanas* differ, Gaṅgā being characterised by a *makara* and Yamunā by a tortoise. Moreover, the earlier figures are each overshadowed by a tree, but the fluvial goddesses portrayed on the later temples usually carry the appropriate emblems of the lotus-flower and the water-vessel.

The following observations will help to explain these points of difference.[1] The figures in question are undoubtedly the prototypes of the medieval images of the two sacred rivers, but on the other hand they are evidently derived from the curious brackets carved with a female holding on to the branch of a tree which not only decorate the *toraṇas* of Sānchi, but which were also employed in the art of Mathurā, where they must have had the same function. The figures of Mathurā are placed on various *vāhanas* including the *makara*, and there can be little doubt that, like the earlier examples from Sānchi, they represent Yakshiṇīs. Not only is there the great similarity between those cariatids of early Buddhist art and the female figures of the Gupta period which we are discussing. But also the position of the latter on both sides of the architrave of the doorway and the peculiar shape of the projecting panel which they occupy find their explanation in the circumstance

(1) For a more detailed treatment of the point in question the author may refer to his paper *Gaṅgā et Yamunā dans l'iconographie brahmanique. Études Asiatiques, publiées à l'occasion du 25e anniversaire de l'École Française d'Extrême-Orient,* vol. II pp. 385 ff.

that the motif was originally employed in connection with the *toraṇa* brackets.

The figures, as we find them at Ajaṇṭā and Bagh, represent therefore a transitional stage between the Yakshiṇīs of early Buddhist art and the fluvial goddesses found in the Brahmanical temples of medieval India. But whether at this stage they still retain their original meaning or have already received their novel significance it is difficult to make out with full certainty. The former alternative seems indeed to be the more probable, because, as has been remarked above, these figures which are both raised on a *makara* and canopied by a tree, have preserved an aspect similar to that of the bracket figures of Sānchi and Mathurā. It was no doubt their vehicle which suggested a connection with the two twin rivers of Madhyadeśa, for the *makara* is the aquatic animal *par excellence*. Says Kṛishṇa in the *Bhagavadgītā* (X, 31): "Among fishes I am the *makara* and among rivers the Ganges." But it is only in the later Gupta architecture represented by the temples of Deogaṛh and Tigowa, that the two female doorkeepers are distinguished by their *vāhanas*, the *makara* and the tortoise, and consequently can be identified with full certainty as the personifications of the two sacred rivers, Gaṅgā and Yamunā.

In the face of the rock intervening between Caves No. 5 and 6, there are traces of four figures in a row. Nothing more than the shoulders and arms of these figures now remains. Similarly the chapel at the south-western end of the portico of Cave No. 7 contains two damaged figures on its rear wall and a third figure on its left side wall. These figures are too fragmentary to be identified.

II Paintings

The best preserved portion of the Bagh paintings is found on the outer surface of the front wall of Caves No. 4 and 5.[1] Along these caves there was originally a continuous verandah, 220 ft. in length, supported by a row of some twenty heavy pillars which have now almost entirely disappeared. The rock which formed the roof of this verandah has also collapsed with the result that the upper half of the wall on which the paintings are found has become exposed to the weather, except where protected by the overhanging rock. The lower half of the wall was entirely concealed from view by the fallen débris, but after these had been removed by the Archæological Department of Gwalior State, it was found that everywhere the painted layer of *chunam* had vanished, probably owing to the action of the rain water. Along the upper half of the wall the paintings are still extant but in a state far from perfect. Large portions have completely disappeared. What remains shows considerable gaps and the colours have in places become so faint that it is only possible to make out the outline of the paintings by sprinkling the surface with water. Visitors have added to the general havoc by the abominable practice of scribbling their names all over the remaining portion of the paintings. In consequence of the very fragmentary state of the paintings we have not succeeded in identifying the particular story to which they refer. All we can say is that they do not appear to illustrate any subject taken from the Buddha legend but in all probability relate to some *jātaka* or *avadāna*.

---

(1) Cave No. 4 has three doorways and two windows. The best preserved portion of the paintings is found on the wall surface from the right hand or southern door of cave No. 4 up to where cave No. 5 commences.

A somewhat detailed description will perhaps help to elucidate the meaning of these interesting paintings.

We commence our description from the right hand (southern most) doorway of Cave No. 4. Over it we notice two scenes, of which the first one is very indistinct (Plate A). Two women seated in an open pavilion can be distinguished, of whom the one is evidently overpowered with grief. With her right hand she covers her face, whilst the left hand, finely drawn, is held out in a very telling gesture. The other lady has the attitude of a sympathetic partner of her sorrows and appears to be engaged in comforting her or in listening to her tale of woe. She rests her head in her left hand, the wrist of which is encircled with two bracelets. On the roof of the pavilion there are traces of two pairs of birds, apparently blue pigeons.[1]

In the second scene (Plate B) four personages, all males presumably and of a very dark complexion, are evidently engaged in a very serious discussion, as indicated by the expression of their faces as well as by the position of their hands. Each of them sits cross-legged on a round, blue and white cushion, and wears no other garment but a striped *dhotī*. The four form, as it were, two groups, each of two, those on the left being turned halfway towards those on the right. The one who is second from the left hand side must be a personage of superior rank, either a king or a deity, to judge from his high and elaborate head-dress which is square in shape and beset with jewels. The person sitting behind him likewise wears a crown which, however, is different in form. Besides, both these figures wear ornaments consisting of a

(1) In the school scene of Ajaṇṭā, too, the artist has enlivened the picture by means of birds sitting on the roof. Cf. *Ajaṇṭā Paintings*, pl. 45

double necklace, bracelets round the upper arms, and bangles round the wrists. The chief person with the high mitre has also ear-rings. The two remaining persons are simpler in appearance, as Dr. Impey rightly remarks, although not wholly devoid of ornaments. The third one has a bare head, but his companion seated at his left side, who is somewhat smaller in size, appears to wear a diadem. There is a fifth figure, of blue colour—it must be either a child or a dwarf—which is distinguished by a curious white crest, trefoil-shaped, on the top of its head. It is seated in front of the left-hand couple. The scene, whatever its meaning may be, is laid in a garden, park or forest. This may be concluded from the background which shows remnants of foliage indicative of trees.

The third scene (Plate C) consists of two distinct groups of figures placed the one over the other. Whether these two groups belong together and in reality form one scene, it is impossible to decide, as long as the subject of these frescoes has not been identified. The upper group consists of six (Dr. Impey says five) male figures evidently flying and issuing forth from the clouds. This is in particular clear from the person who seems to head the company and from the position in which he holds his legs. The lower half of the left leg of this figure is plainly visible, the foot being partly concealed behind the head of one of the persons of the lower group. Of the right leg only a small portion above the knee is shown, the rest being hidden by the clouds. The dress of this figure consists merely of a lower garment or *dhotī*. In the case of the remaining personages of this group only the upper half of the body above the waist is shown, the remainder disappearing behind the clouds. They wear a white or greenish upper garment which covers the left shoulder but leaves the right shoulder bare. These flying figures are moving towards the right of the spectator with hands stretched forth, the open palm being turned upwards, as if to receive or to bestow some gift or blessing. Or can it be that they shower flowers on the group beneath? The first figure on the right hand side which unfortunately is very indistinct seems to carry in one hand a tray or flat basket containing white and blue flowers. As these figures do not wear any ornaments and have shaven heads, they possibly represent *arhats* or *ṛishis* transporting themselves through the air, as is the usual practice of such privileged beings.

Of the group beneath only five heads are preserved, apparently belonging to female musicians, as the one in the centre holds a musical instrument which may be either a guitar or a lute (Skt. *vīṇā*). The women have their hair brushed back off the forehead and tied in a knot at the back of their head; the fourth one has hers dressed with a white ribbon and blue flowers. All of them seem to wear a close fitting bodice, that worn by the central figure is green dotted over with white, whilst that of the last one standing at the right side is blue. They wear moreover ear-rings, some jewelled, and necklaces of pearls interspersed with larger stones of blue colour. Dr. Impey calls them turquoises, but the shade seems to agree more with the darker hue of lapis lazuli.

We now come to the fourth scene (Plate D) consisting of a double group of female musicians.[1] The left hand group comprises seven women standing around an eighth figure, evidently

(1) It is interesting to compare the group of six female musicians around a dancing-girl which is found in cave No. 1 of Ajaṇṭā, the instruments being partly the same. *Cf. Ajaṇṭā Paintings*, pl. 6.

a dancer, who wears a peculiar kind of costume. It is a long-sleeved tunic greenish with white dots reaching down to the knees, a loose girdle, and a broad flat kind of collar over which a necklace of pearls interspersed with large beads of lapis lazuli is visible. Sleek locks fall down on both his or her shoulders. The legs are clothed in striped trousers set wide apart, the right one being bent. The palms of the hands are turned upwards in the position assumed by dancing-girls. Two bracelets encircle each wrist. The head, which is thrown somewhat back, is covered with a kind of scarf, white coloured with blue stripes.

Of the seven musicians one plays a tabor or hand-drum, three have each two little sticks, and three hold cymbals. The one with the hand-drum (Skt. *mṛidaṅga*) is nude down to the waist. Her instrument hangs on her left side in a sling. The two hands with fingers moving in the act of striking the leather are well rendered. The knot of hair at the back of the head is held together by means of a wreath of white flowers. The next one standing to her right a little further back wears a kind of scarf thrown over her left shoulder and leaving the breast partly uncovered. Her left wrist is provided with three bangles. The next three musicians are each engaged in beating a pair of wooden sticks called *ḍaṇḍā* in Hindī and *ṭipri* in Marāṭhī.

The remaining three beat small-sized cymbals which are known as *mañjira* in Hindī and as *tāḷā* (from Skt. *tāla*) in Marāṭhī. Among the three last mentioned the one occupying the centre is clad in a short-sleeved bodice (Marāṭhī *choli*) of blue colour. The one on her left wears a greenish garment with sleeves reaching down to the wrists. The musician in front on the left end of the group is nude down to the hips, the lower half of her body being clothed in a striped garment of three colours—white, blue, and green. In front of the group we notice a bench or couch on which a blue-striped white cushion of cylindrical form is laid.

The second group of female musicians (Plate E) is likewise arrayed round a dancer with long black locks, who is clad in a long green tunic and striped trousers and wears ear-rings and bangles. Of the six women one beats a tabor, two handle small-sized cymbals, and three each a pair of sticks. The one standing behind the central figure has a green upper-garment leaving her body partly exposed, and a striped under-garment. Her neighbour wears a green scarf thrown across her left shoulder, and the next one a yellowish bodice cut out over her throat. The three remaining musicians are nude down to the waist.

The scene here described is separated from the next one to the right by means of a partition which presents the appearance of a green coloured wall with a white coping angularly placed. Beneath this partition there are remnants of an inscription which appears to have consisted of two lines of writing in the Gupta character. Only one letter is plainly visible, it is a looped *ka*, apparently the concluding letter of the first line. In front of it there are traces of another letter which can no longer be identified, but seems to be provided with the vowel-mark *e*.

Possibly this inscription refers to the subject of the fifth scene (Plate F) which portrays a cavalcade of at least seventeen[(1)] horsemen moving towards the left in five or six rows. The principal personage must be the cavalier in the centre over whose

(1) Dr. Impey, op. cit, p. 563, speaks of thirteen.

head a parasol, the emblem of royalty, appears. He is clad in a blue-dotted, yellowish robe and holds the reins of his bay steed[1] with his left hand. The horse carries three yak-tails (Skt. *chāmara*), one standing on the top of the head and two hanging down along the head and the neck. These typical ornaments are not only regularly found in the sculptures of Sānchi, where royal processions are pictured and likewise in the paintings of Ajaṇṭā,[2] but they are also referred to in Sanskrit literature. We need only recall the beginning of the first act of Kālidāsa's *Śakuntalā*, where the charioteer of King Dushyanta in describing the speed of the chariot speaks of the waving plumes which now stand motionless on the top of the horses' heads. It is curious that in the painting under discussion the yak-tails are decidedly blue, whereas the natural colour of these objects can only be white and black. The question arises whether this can be the colour originally applied by the artist or whether in the course of time the original colour has become changed. The latter alternative seems the more probable as the Bagh paintings present other instances in which this same blue colour occurs associated with objects which in reality can hardly have been blue, such as cymbals, a horse's saddle, and a bow.

On the right side of the principal and probably royal figure described above there rides another person of rank mounted on a red-brown horse, his green tunic all dotted over with yellow. Over him we notice a man seated on a dark green horse which turns its head sideways. The rider wears a yellowish robe, the

(1) Dr. Impey says that he is seated on a white horse "which colour appears to have been thus early, as it is still, considered an emblem of superiority with Buddhists."

(2) From the Ajaṇṭā paintings it is evident that the horses used to carry four chowries, namely, one on the top of the head, two on both sides of the head, and one hanging down under the chin. Cf. *Ajaṇṭā Frescoes*, fig. 22, plates 66, 67, 68, and 72, and *Ajaṇṭā Frescoes*, pl. VIII, XVIII, XXII, and XLII.

horse a golden *chāmara*. Between this horseman and the partition wall the head of a man and that of a horse, both remarkably well drawn, are still traceable.

To the left of the chief personage there rides a man in a yellowish robe, who raises his right hand while his left holds the reins. His horse of reddish brown colour carries a blue saddle and a white saddle cloth.

The man next to him in the foreground, whose horse is lost, presents a peculiar appearance. He is distinguished by a ruddy complexion and by sleek black hair. His costume consists of an ochre-coloured coat and of a yellow cap relieved by little blue ornaments.

The vanguard is supplied by a row of three figures; their horses have well-nigh completely disappeared. The man occupying the right end of the row, who is clad in a yellow robe and carries a blue-coloured bow, has apparently no horse and seems to be a foot-soldier. Of the two horsemen the one to the proper right holds his head slightly bent. He wears a yellow tunic enlivened with little ornaments somewhat resembling birds in shape. He wears jewelled ear-rings, as seems to be the case with all the figures in this group, as far as can be ascertained. The outline of the head of his horse can still be traced.

The third row consists of four horsemen. The cavalier in front (*viz.*: on the proper left end of the row) rides a reddish steed adorned with two chowries, the one standing on the top of the head and the other hanging down in front of the neck. His neighbour, who is dressed in a blue tunic and yellow trousers, is evidently engaged in pulling up his brown horse which slightly turns its head round. The person riding to his right wears a yellow robe dotted over with little lozenges. The fourth horseman on the right end of the row is clad in blue, but here the colouring has become extremely faint.

The rear is formed by three riders: the first clad in a yellowish robe is seated on a brown horse, the next one in a robe of the same colour on a green horse, and the third dressed in blue on a bay steed.

All the personages forming this stately cavalcade wear long-sleeved tunics reaching halfway down the thigh, and a curious kind of head-dress hanging down from the back of the head, usually white or yellowish of colour and sometimes relieved with blue flowerets. It is a point worthy of notice that in this composition the artist has rendered his horses with great feeling for the noble character of these animals.(1) This is the more remarkable as in general the Indian sculptor does not excel in this respect. Not only in Indian sculpture, but also in the wonderful bas-reliefs of Borobudur, the horses are stiff and lifeless.

The elephant, on the contrary, we always find portrayed with great vigour throughout Indian art both sculptural and pictorial. Let us only quote the various renderings of the birth-story of the six-tusked elephant (*Chaddanta-jātaka*) found in the sculptures of Sānchi and in the paintings of Ajaṇṭā. Among the latter there is also the charming story of the young elephant, the devoted son of his blind mother who, when captured, refuses to take any food until set at liberty again by the king's order (*Mātuposaka-jātaka*).(2)

---

(1) Cf. Dr. Impey's remarks, op. cit., p. 563. (2) Cf. *Ajaṇṭā Frescoes*, pl. XIX, XX, XXI, and XXVII.

The same talent in characterizing the most typical animal in Indian life is plainly noticeable in the sixth scene (Plates G-I) which represents an elephant procession. It is separated from the cavalcade described above by means of a rocky wall,(1) the rocks being rendered in the same conventional manner as is the case at Ajaṇṭā. The present group, according to Dr. Impey's description, consists of six elephants and three horsemen. Of the latter only one is now traceable.

The elephant heading the procession has almost entirely gone, only the outline of the head being still visible. Its rider is a personage of very striking appearance, (Plate H) distinguished by his large size, tawny complexion and long, sleek locks of black colour. He wears a white cap decorated with what looks like little blue flowers. He is naked down to the waist; a short *dhotī* striped blue and white is partly preserved. His raised right hand holds the long stalk of a blue flower which has almost entirely gone. Dr. Impey calls it an open lotus-flower. His elephant is covered with a housing (Hindī *jhūl*) ochre-coloured and dotted. Notwithstanding his scanty dress, this quaint elephant-rider must be a person of royal rank, as an attendant in a close fitting coat seated behind him holds the two emblems of royalty—the chowrie or fly-whisk (Skt. *chāmara*) made of the tail of the yak, and the umbrella (Skt. *chhattra*, *ātapatra*). In his right hand this satellite waves the chowrie of reddish colour, and with his left he grasps the long staff of the parasol which he holds over the head of the royal personage seated in front of him. A wreath hangs down from

(1) Dr. Impey calls it "a castellated portal." But this conventional way of rendering a rocky landscape occurs regularly not only in Indian art but also elsewhere. Cf. *Ajaṇṭā Frescoes*, pl. 14, 19, 21, 31, 32, 57, 60, 63, 74, 80, 83, 86, and *Ajaṇṭā Frescoes*, pl. II, V, VI*b*, VIII, XI, XXIII, XXV, XXXII, XXXIII, XXXVIII*b*, and XXXIX*b*.

the last-mentioned emblem, as is regularly the case with the parasols surmounting the *stūpas* in the reliefs of Sānchi and Mathurā.

Immediately behind this parasol-bearer there appears a brown horse with white trappings and reins, carrying a floating chowrie between its ears. The horseman clad in an ochre-coloured tunic has almost entirely vanished. Dr. Impey says that he wears a turban being "the only one covered in the whole series," but nothing of it now remains. Only his nose and right eye are still visible, and his two hands, one of which holds the reins.

The central portion of this scene is formed by four elephants, two large and two smaller ones, apparently walking in a row and following the royal personage who rides in front. One of the small elephants has advanced beyond the line, the *mahaut* trying to restrain the animal by means of his blue-striped spud or crook (Skt. *aṅkuśa*). The two large elephants are each mounted by one man without such an instrument. In either case a second male figure is visible behind the elephant's back. Evidently this second person is not mounted on the elephant nor can he be supposed to be walking, unless we are to assume some fault in drawing. Is he hanging on to the elephant's trappings ?

Both these attendants carry a staff in their right hand which may belong to a banner, flag, or lance. Dr. Impey calls it a banner, but at present nothing is left but the stick.

The enormous tusker whose huge head is conspicuous in the centre of the composition has large tusks, tipped with blue. The colour of his skin is greenish with a lighter shade on his head and trunk. The smaller elephant in the foreground, and another immediately above forming the rear-guard of the procession carry each a *mahaut* and three female figures (Plate I). The *mahaut* on the one in front holds the usual crook in both hands. He is naked down to the hips and wears a short *dhotī* striped white and blue. His left leg is concealed behind the elephant's ear. Of the three females two are seated astride, whereas the third one is shown kneeling and catching hold of her companion who seems to look round at her. The first and third ones are nude down to the waist, the one in the centre wears a short-sleeved, white bodice open at the breast. They are clothed in *dhotīs* striped white and green and wear the usual ornaments—ear-rings, necklaces of large beads or pearls alternating with blue stones, bracelets, and foot-rings round the ankles. The elephant which they are riding is covered with a housing ochre-coloured dotted over with white flowerets.

A similar group of four figures is mounted on the elephant in the back-ground. Here the first and third of the three females wear a short-sleeved bodice, the second one does not. They all wear striped *dhotīs*. The second and third ones have an object resembling a tabour hanging on their left side. The former wears a string of pearls with a large-sized bead of lapis lazuli in the centre. Their elephant is covered with a housing with broad stripes of blue and light greenish colour.

The elephant procession is separated from the seventh and last scene by means of a building with a curvilinear and gabled roof, apparently a gateway. Gateways of this type are often met with in the Ajaṇṭā paintings.[1]

---

(1) *Ajaṇṭā Frescoes*, pl. 6, 16, 28, 58, 66, 67, and 69. *Ajaṇṭā Frescoes*, pl. XVII, XXIV, XXIX, and XLII*b*.

The paintings on the right hand or southern side of this shrine were still visible at the time of Dr. Impey's visit to the Bagh Caves. As at present they have almost entirely disappeared, our best plan will be to quote that writer's description. "The next [scene]" he says, "is a peculiar and interesting group, facing exactly the contrary direction, and consisting of four elephants and three horses, which seem to have arrived at their destination. The elephants are at rest, and the mahouts quietly reposing, their heads on their arms crossed on the crown of the elephant's heads, which animals are looking steadfastly to their front, as are the horses; one of the former carries a checked garment in his trunk. There are two avant footmen with swords and spears. Like the rest, they have their attention fixed on the substance in the compartment in advance, which commences with the famous Amb, bo or mango tree, under which are two small frames or stands containing some drinking vessels and a gourd. Close to these a piece of cloth with blue ends is suspended from a branch and beside it is a Chakra or praying wheel."

"Further on under the shade of a plantain tree is a figure of Buddh, seated cross-legged and clothed, holding the thumb of his right hand in his left, and beside him a disciple listening to the doctrine he is expounding. He differs from Buddhist figures in general in being *without* curly hair, and in this respect resembles the other figures met with. A door breaks the further continuation of figures in this direction, and beyond it the surface of the wall is entirely broken up."

Of the paintings seen by Dr. Impey hardly anything now remains plainly visible. By moistening the surface it is possible to bring out a few more traces of the vanished frescoes on this part of the wall. A brief survey will show how little is left. Over the gabled building which, as we have seen, serves as a means of separation, enough still remains to identify a very fine, large-sized elephant with big, blue-tipped tusks and light-coloured straps. It is mounted by two men, the one being the *mahaut* with his *aṅkus* at rest, and the other squatting behind. Two more elephants can be faintly discerned. Further on the well-drawn head of a horse which, like the elephants, is turned towards the right can still be made out and perhaps the outline of a second horse.

On the remaining portion of the wall the stem of a tree as well as the presence of foliage seems to indicate that the scene is laid in a park or garden. Dr. Impey, as we have seen, mentions a mango-tree in this part of the paintings.

Near the upper corner of the window it is possible to trace two figures perhaps representing ascetics or monks. The one to the proper right is fairly distinct, his head in particular being well preserved. He is dressed in a white upper garment with long sleeves; his undergarment, too, is white-coloured but relieved by little blue adornments. He is seated cross-legged, his right hand being raised in front of his breast and the left resting in his lap. This is perhaps the personage whom Dr. Impey describes as "a figure of Buddh" seated under a plantain tree. If so, the proposed identification cannot be correct, as the figure in question does not show the characteristic marks of the Buddha. In fact, Dr. Impey himself notes the absence of the curly hair generally associated with the Master. From the little that is left of the second person (only one hand and part of the face can still be distinguished) it is evident that he sat turned towards the personage first described.

Between these two figures and the group of elephants and horses there is a white gateway apparently giving access to the garden. The upper portion of the fresco shows the foliage of trees. It is with the greatest difficulty that we can still make out the stands carrying rounded vessels and gourds of various hue which are included in Dr. Impey's description.

To the north of the central doorway of the *vihāra* Cave, No. 4, there are some faint traces of frescoes which even at the time of Dr. Impey's visit were indistinct, although their state of preservation appears then to have been slightly better than it is now. "They are now," that author wrote, "in such fragmental portions that it was found impossible to take a connected sketch, and all between the first and central doors are utterly defaced. The best remnants are near the extreme north door, and even they are not distinct, except a few figures here and there, which are much smaller, though some few are of full length but in miniature. Similar to the other pieces, it has been divided into an upper and lower row, the feet of one resting almost on the heads of the other. The aspect of the representation is contrary to the former, viz. southward, towards the remains of a colossal figure of Buddha, the outlines of which can be traced indistinctly sitting in a garden between the first window and chief door. The commencement of the upper row resembles the healing of the sick: one lean man is sitting and another lying down, their limbs emaciated, while a third seems to be carried before a fourth figure, who appears to be advising them."

"Two females next occur in a mourning attitude, preceded by a child in glee; then four dancing figures, and another child running, but looking backwards; this borders on the figure of Buddh referred to. The lower row is excessively indistinct, the heads only being traceable satisfactorily; none can be counted: there is one, however, a female with a child at her feet, evidently praying to the figure of Buddh above described. Among the foliage, flowers, etc., surrounding Buddh, one or two contemplative heads are also seen."

It is extremely difficult to guess from the passage quoted what the meaning of the paintings here described can have been. We cannot even be certain about the identity of the "colossal figure of Buddh" noted by Dr. Impey, as in the course of his paper he applies the term "figure of Buddh" to images which clearly do not represent Buddha at all, such as the rock-cut Nāga and Yaksha figures placed in recesses outside the monasteries. The figure in question may, therefore, quite well have been a Bodhisattva or even a Yaksha. Unfortunately we lack the means of checking Dr. Impey's account, as at present hardly any trace of these frescoes remains. Only the halo of the supposed Buddha image is still faintly visible. It must have been a large figure, probably standing, and perhaps was one out of a pair of Bodhisattvas flanking the doorway, such as we find on both sides of the entrance to the sanctuary of the *Vihāra* Cave, No. 1, of Ajaṇṭā. At the side of the halo but a little higher, on the same level with the sculptured female image on the *makara* which decorates the door frame, there are faint vestiges of a figure apparently seated cross-legged and turned towards the door. Over the halo there appears to have been a pair of *kinnaras*, one with a guitar, apparently standing on the back of the Buddha's or Bodhisattva's throne.

At the right side of the entrance to the inner shrine three large size figures are partly preserved. In front is a standing female figure with large ear-rings and head bent in reverence and with her eyes half closed in devotion. The central figure is a male whose shoulders and hands alone are now visible. The third figure at the back is a corpulent figure, perhaps a Yaksha, of which only a portion of the torso remains.

Some good floral and foliated scrolls are faintly visible on the back row of pillars in Cave No. 4. The decorative frieze which once ran round the walls of this *vihāra* has been partly preserved. It consists of an undulating course of stems of lotus plants with leaves, buds and flowers, interspersed with various kinds of fruits, birds, animals and human figures. The paintings which decorated the ceilings of this as well as of other caves have wellnigh completely vanished. As in the case of Ajaṇṭā they mostly consisted of squares inset with birds, animals and bunches of leaves and fruits and in some cases, of concentric circles (Plates XVI-XVIII).

The central cell of the outer group of five cells in Cave No. 3 was originally decorated with figures of Buddhas and perhaps Bodhisattvas of which only the haloes remain. In one instance the head with the *ushnīsha* and part of the robe covering both shoulders is preserved. The back-ground is decorated with white flowers. The walls of the central cell of the inner group of five cells were likewise decorated with Buddha figures standing on lotuses and surrounded with oval-shaped haloes. The lotus with the well-drawn feet of one of these figures, and a worshipper kneeling and holding in his right hand the handle of a lamp, and in his left hand some unidentified object are still seen. Faint traces of figures flanking the entrance of this cell are also visible. A figure stooping and stretching the right hand to the ground is seen on the left side of the entrance.

NOTES ON THE PAINTINGS

By E. B. HAVELL

The very precious fragments of the grand school of Indian mural painting here illustrated are in one respect unique; for not even at Ajanta is there found a similar scene conceived on so large a scale and designed with so much freedom and spaciousness. The main subject is a city pageant or festival, such as may be witnessed to-day in Rajputana and many other parts of India. The dominating motive of the decorative scheme is a royal procession with elephants and a splendid cavalcade of nobles, gaily dressed. They move together over some twenty feet of wall in a grand sweeping curve. The minor groups, including a very delightful group of dancers, who appear to be performing on the terraced roof of a building, are subordinate to the chief motif. It is the skill with which the artist has preserved the due relation between the major and minor parts of his design, and welded them together into a rich and harmonious whole, with no apparent effort or straining after effect, which entitle this great Bagh painting to be ranked among the highest achievements of its class.

Unfortunately, the scale of the painting and the subject itself do not lend themselves to reproduction in ordinary book-form. The necessity of showing the painting in sections, and thus breaking up its artistic unity, gives the impression of a gallery of modern cabinet pictures instead of a single masterpiece of a great school of mural painting. However, the reader who studies carefully the key-plate, joining the upper half on the lower one, end-to-end, will be able to understand how the great picture, or what remains of it, hangs together.

In the reproductions of the very careful and sympathetic copies made by Mr. A. K. Haldar and his associates, Plates D and E, showing the bevy of girl-musicians with the two male dancers in their midst, will attract most attention for the perfect design of the whole group, expressing in a wreath of interwoven line and form the rhythm and music of the dance. The peculiar coiffure of the two dancers suggests a comparison with the famous Chola images of the Nataraja. In these images Siva's hair is spread out in separate wavy locks on either side of his head in a similar fashion to that of the two Bagh dancers, except that the latter have not, apparently, learnt the mystery of a permanent wave. Are the Bagh dancers performing the dance of the cosmic rhythm, and was this peculiar coiffure the traditional mode for male dancers who performed the great dance of Siva? In the temples of Southern India the dance is now, I think, only performed by the Devadasis; but very probably the original tradition of the male dancers survives somewhere, as it seems to be represented at Bagh.

It must not be supposed that modern hand-copies of the classics of Indian painting represent the wonderful technique of the Old Masters. Their marvellous sureness and expressiveness of brushline, and the skill and subtlety with which they modelled surfaces, can only be understood from the very best photographic reproductions. Thus from an artistic point of view a perfect photographic reproduction is much more valuable than the best copy which modern artists can furnish. Such copies are very useful as supplements to the exact records of the scientific photographer, but they can never be satisfactory substitutes for them.

For this reason it is to be hoped that the too-long-delayed photographic survey of all the priceless fragments of India's greatest pictorial art, including those illustrated in this book, will be put in hand as a duty which our generation owes to posterity.

AESTHETICAL

By JAMES H. COUSINS, D.Lit.

I paid a visit to the Bagh Caves in January, 1925, in the good company of the Superintendent of Archæology of Gwalior State, Mr. M. B. Garde, B.A., for the purpose of gaining an impression of the frescoes *in situ* and writing of them from the aesthetical point of view. But the association between painting and sculpture in the great era of Indian art, of which Bagh is so valuable an example, was aesthetically so close that it is impossible to avoid some reference to the plastic aspect of the excavated chambers.

The old artists were masters of expressional form. This, both in painting and sculpture, is attained through the special use of the *line* which not only separates space from space but reveals the emotion of the circumstances that have brought such spaces together. Moreover, in giving emotional voice to both pictorial and plastic vision (which is art's miracle of making the dumb speak), the artist's own creative joy flows into his line and directs its flow. From this arises the freedom of movement that is seen in the lines. From it arises also a rhythmical quality that shows itself in the repetition (with a difference) of themes in design like recurrent phrases in music or poetry ; and in the postures of the figures both in the frescoes and sculptures—a certain bend of body as though it had floated into shape on waves of an invisible sea.

Everywhere in the classical era of Indian art one gets this

direct touch from the life of the artist—the sign and token of an art that is not yet at the crest whence the day of its decadence can be sighted. Yet the artists, who come to us in a subtle tangibility, are unknown. Their glorious work stands before us in the paradox of an art that is at once intimately personal and devoid of the "taint of personality."

Happily for the student of Indian artistic form, the general destruction which a millennium-and-a-half of time and desertion has brought to Bagh has still left a number of impressive sculptural groups; but to these other writers will refer, and we now turn to the paintings.

The first accessible cave is not at the moment approachable, as the space in front, once the covered verandah, is being brushed for the coming of boys and girls of the local aboriginal Bhils to the "school" which has been provided for them in such romantic surroundings by His Highness the Maharaja of Gwalior. But there are other caves that call us and begin the subtle conquest of the imagination. In a small and lightless cell (which we illuminate with electric torches) a pair of exquisitely painted feet of the Buddha are of such compelling quality that one is touched with a curious sense of exasperated futility at not being able to see or recreate the vanished figure. One chafes at the irresistible power of decay, and longs to turn back the wheels of the Cosmos in order to recover the great moment of that expression of devotion and beauty.

Elsewhere, on the ceilings of cells and passages, there are challenging traces of fresco designs associating all the kingdoms of animate nature with the general social and devotional idea that co-ordinates the entire decorative scheme of Bagh. Some of these are clear, but most of them have been smoked out of existence by the fires of generations of recluses of an era later than that of the paintings, a time in which the aesthetical sensibility of India suffered the partial eclipse whose penumbra is still upon her though happily cadent. One observes in these ceiling tablets the same freedom with nature as is seen in the paintings, a psychological perspective taking the place of the supposed perspective of the eye. An insect must share in the festival of artistic devotion; it must therefore submit to enlargement in order to fill its allotted space. An elephant *per contra* must be content with microscopic proportions. The same principle is seen in the deep frieze of scroll-work that apparently ran round the great Rangmahal (colour hall), and must have given to the regal dimensions and the sense of power in its forest of great pillars the counterbalance of unity and delicacy. Here the rhythmic element is at its highest, sweeping the kingdoms of nature into its vortices of joy, asking only that they be content, without the precedence of quantity, to take their place in the onward sweep of the *Ananda* (bliss) of creation. Here painting, poetry and music are one.

In the centre of the great verandah, we turn our attention to the precious fragment of forty-five feet out of the original two hundred and twenty feet of wall that bore the paintings which will cause Bagh to be remembered for all time, even though what yet remains should itself disappear. The first look, as we mount the heap of debris that lifts us to the level of the painting, brings disappointment. The end of our quest is a speckled area of unintelligibility. Yet it has some curious attraction of mystery.

Suddenly the eye perceives dimly an exquisitely postured hand. Another ghostly shape emerges out of nothing—a shadowy head touched with the faint aroma of an antique courtesy; then—a finely moulded foot—a horse's neck gloriously arched—the monumental forehead of a state elephant. One after another, like stars in twilight, they take the eye, these points of dim radiance on the darkening sky of history, moving the heart with a solemn joy, and stirring the imagination to discovery until there stretches before the inner eye the recreated pageant of a vanished life, even as the celestial mystery of the zodiac took form in the imaginations of the ancients around a few fixed points in the unfathomable abyss of night.

To the hazard of the imagination certainty and fulness are given when water is thrown on the now articulate wall. Instantly there comes forth a vivid and crowded life depicted with such mastery that one forgets for the time the depiction and is absorbed in the life. One moves this way or that with one or other of the two festal processions that formed the subject of the portion of the painting that time has left us. There is a surge of longing to know the cause of the sorrow of the weeping lady to whom another lady gives apparently unavailing comfort, or to hear the message of the spirit which is being uttered by the quiet teacher to his absorbed pupils. We pause to reflect that much of the vivid reality of the picture comes from the acute psychology of the artist, who poses his figures in such manner that we are graciously admitted to their company; yet neither our presence nor our departure can disturb them, or deflect them from their complete interest in their own concerns . . . But the call of time is insistent; the revelation of the past fades out slowly but inexorably, leaving us with a feeling of vast bereavement, but leaving us also, for consolation, with the realisation that always comes in the presence of supreme expressions of man's reaction to the creative impulse of the Cosmic life, that in great art there is no ancient and no modern, but only the contemporaneousness of eternal life and truth.

Fortunately, the wisdom of a Prince and the skill of modern artists have preserved for us the copies of the Bagh frescoes now published in this volume which art-lovers in all lands and through the ages to come will treasure as an invaluable presentation of a hitherto vaguely-known phase of the classical art of India. Set alongside the reproductions of the Ajanta frescoes in an equally precious companion volume, they point the way to a comparative study which students in the future will elaborate, but which here we have only space to suggest.

The Bagh frescoes are taken by competent authorities to be contemporaneous with the later Ajanta frescoes. In craftsmanship they are similar. Their mastery over the spontaneous technique of mural painting is no less. They have the same mood of reserve even in the midst of joy. There is no display of egotism, and no triviality. But while the Ajanta frescoes are more religious in theme, depicting incidents from the previous lives of the Buddha with their human associations, the Bagh frescoes are more human, depicting the life of the time with its religious associations. The exquisite austerity of Ajanta tends to obscure the personal element of the artist in the calm depiction of super-personality. But in the Bagh frescoes the humanity of the theme gives free rein to the joy of the artist, though the general tone is one of gracious solemnity. The æsthetical element which is latent, almost cold, in Ajanta, is patent and pulsating in Bagh. A glance of an eye, the poise of a foot, the delicious turn of a hand, and a hundred and one other details of expression and decoration, show the superabundant energy in creation ("a little more and how much it is" beyond the exactly necessary) which bespeaks the flame and expansion of delight.

Art in the highest calls for high objective depiction, for the expression of subjective states of mind and emotion, and for the recognition of the transcendental all-enfolding Life of the Cosmos. These elements are nobly and generously present in sub-divisions and inter-relations in the pictorical presentation of the Bagh paintings, and touch the sensitive observer with the æsthetical sanctification that only the highest art can communicate.

TOPOGRAPHICAL

By JAMES H. COUSINS, D. Lit.

When, and under what circumstances, the last Buddhist monk took his last look at the holy labours of centuries on the walls of the excavated temples of Bagh, we cannot tell, nor whether it was up or down the river valley that his feet went towards Nirvana. But it is not unlikely that, as far as the general features of the environment of this ancient place of religion and art are concerned, things are much the same as they were in the era of their prime, fourteen or more centuries ago.

The choice of situation here, as in similar places like Ajanta, was controlled by circumstances that touched the relatively permanent aspects of nature—temporary seclusion in the season of rain, tempered by some measure of accessibility to the wide fields of religious labour in the season of sunshine; shelter from the elements and wild creatures combined with nearness to food and water. A river-bend and accompanying cliff would serve the purpose, and these time may modify but not soon eliminate. The speculations of humanity in nature's power and variety may have brought details of colour and perfume to the landscape in, perhaps, the blue flax and medicinal thyme; but food and clothing are fundamental, and the rich green that presages the coming gold of the wheat, and the speckled shrubs that promise the snow drift of the cotton, may have been as contributory to human picturesqueness a millennium-and-a-half ago as they are to-day on the road from Mhow to Bagh—ninety miles almost as the crow flies into the south-west corner of the land now happily fathered by a Prince among men, the Maharaja Scindia of Gwalior.(1)

There are other and shorter roads to Bagh than this, but the road from Mhow across the Vindhya Hills adds the lure of speed to the charms of nature. A motor car can be hired for the three days necessary for the excursion, and application in advance will ordinarily secure accommodation in the comfortable inspection bungalow at the town of Bagh.

To reach the excavated temples from the town one walks or travels in a bullock-cart across three miles of cotton-growing land, fording the wriggling river three times on the way. At a point about half-a-mile from our destination we surmount a sharp stony incline and enter a shallow valley across which we see a precipitous and wooded hillside pierced with square holes at a considerable height above the bed of the river. These are some of the entrances to the known eight "caves" that fifteen centuries ago were places of rest and aspiration, study and discipline, for men who gathered here away from the world in order the better to serve it, and who were devoted equally to the art of religion and the religion of art. Our knowledge of the sanctity and artistic glory of the place gives the hush of awe to what the uninformed eye might take to be just a series of apertures neither perfectly plumb nor regularly distributed. Yet in that very imperfection there is the signal of creative movement. The memorials of death may be as mathematically accurate as they please, but life, and art that

(1) This was written more than two years ago (in March, 1925) when His Highness the late Madhava Rao Maharaja Scindia was still in this world of mortals.

is alive, as is all this art of the classical era in India, always shows the asymmetry of spontaneity and fervour, and the touch of imperfection that accompanies the movement of creation from degree to degree of expressional realisation and technical accomplishment.

As a matter of fact, these apertures are not the original entrances as they would have met the eye some centuries ago. They are the inner doors that opened into the excavated chambers from the great verandah. This protection (220 feet from end to end) has now completely disappeared. Nature here has dealt even more harshly with art than ignorant vandalism or neglect. Heat and cold, wind and rain, have applied their erasure to the record of man's effort to lift his own beauty to the comradeship of the invisible beauty. But the root of the matter is deeper than climate. It happened (as one surmises from what is observed on the spot) that the devotees who sought sanctuary at Bagh succumbed to the temptation of a handy section of a bed of soft sandstone which offered comparatively little resistance to hand and implement. In this they unwittingly became accessories to their own intimate defeat, for above the bed of sandstone, into which the sculptors burrowed with an industry that is read even to-day in incalculable chisel marks on the walls, there lies a layer of later rock (clay stone) upwards of 20 feet in thickness. This, it would appear, bears downward on the great spaces of the excavated halls. Yieldings, inappreciable at any particular moment, but cumulatively disastrous, brought down the outer protection of the verandah, and inside the chambers have burst huge pillars even within the past few years of observation. Not a moment too soon did the Department of Archaeology of Gwalior State take up the work of arresting the process of decay ; and it is to be hoped that the operations of clearing the chambers and preserving the precious remnants of India's past which are so intelligently and enthusiastically conducted, will receive all the support necessary to crown them with success.

But if the ancient sculptors did not anticipate geological *karma*, they had a clear eye for situation. The approach to the sacred place had beauty as companion in the general rhythmical contours of the surrounding country. The prospect from the platform in front of the chambers is to-day as the keen eyes of the students and craftsmen must have looked upon it in the days of its glory. The Bagh river murmurs its Precepts eternally along the base of the cliff 30 feet below the " caves." Across the river the shallow valley rises against the skyline dotted with short trees. The ground (for it is the dry season) has the reddish tint that enters so largely into the colour schemes of the pictorial art of Bagh and Ajanta. But in the monsoon season, when the monks would repair to their spiritual home to taste the chastity and peace that still haunt the place like a white Presence, the land would spread before them as green as their memory is to us to-day.

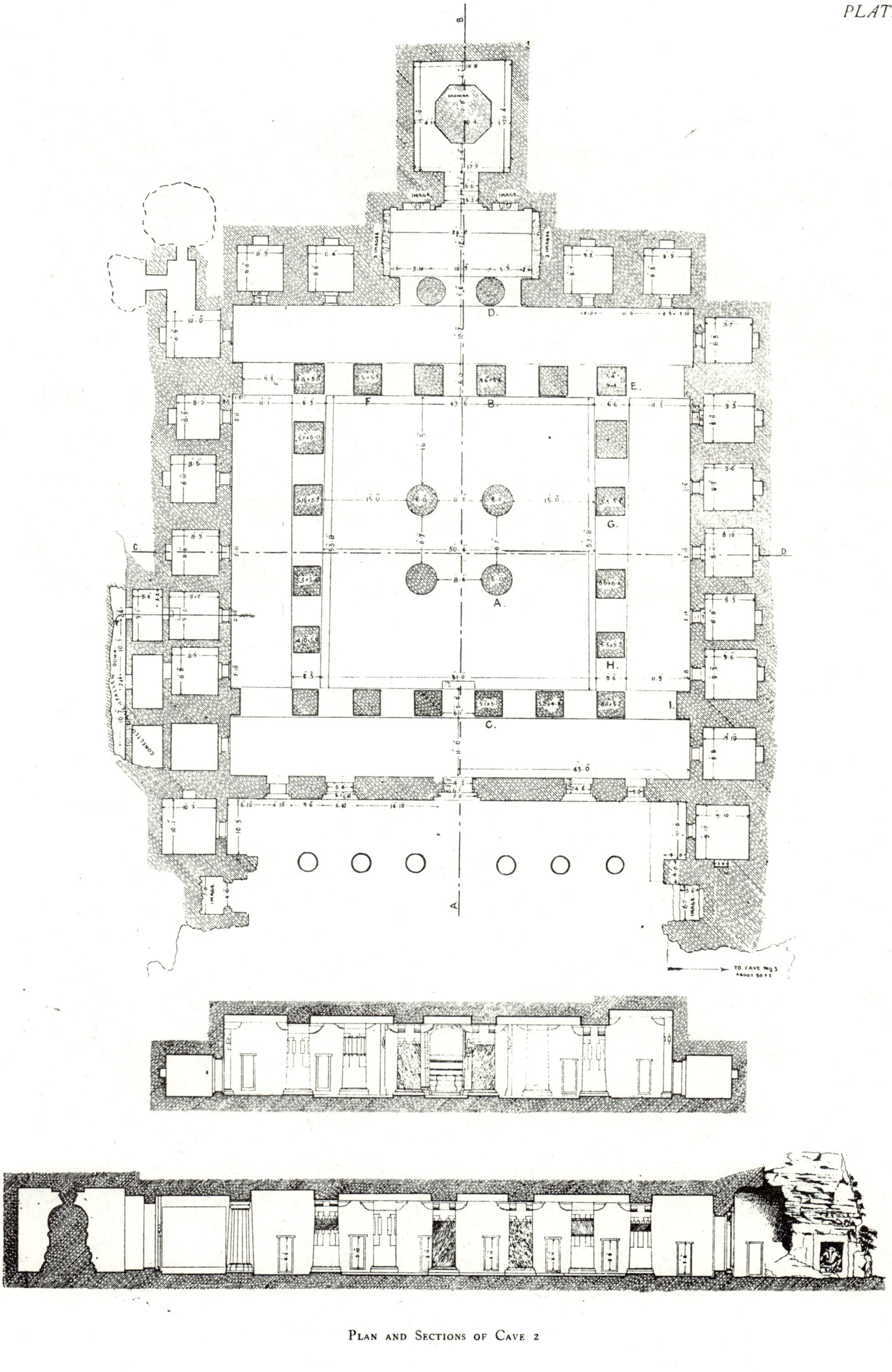

Plan and Sections of Cave 2

a. Facade of Cave 2 at Bagh from S.W.

b. General View of Cave 2

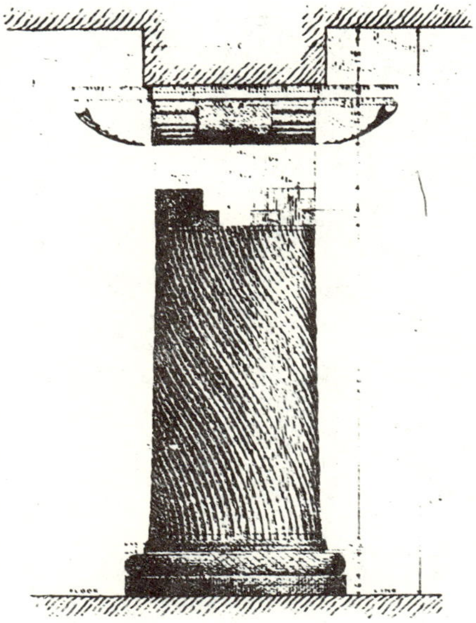

A

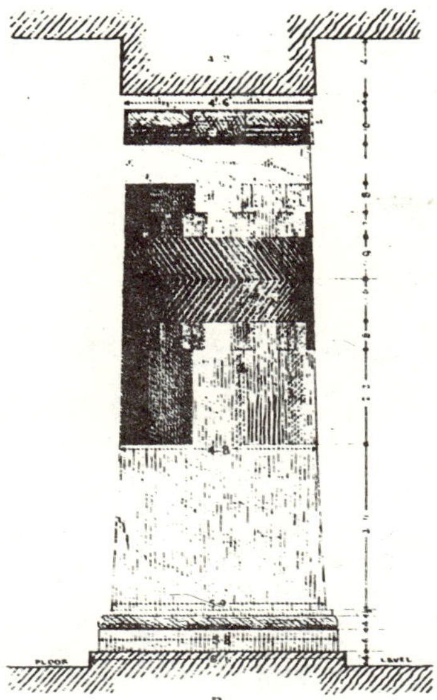

B

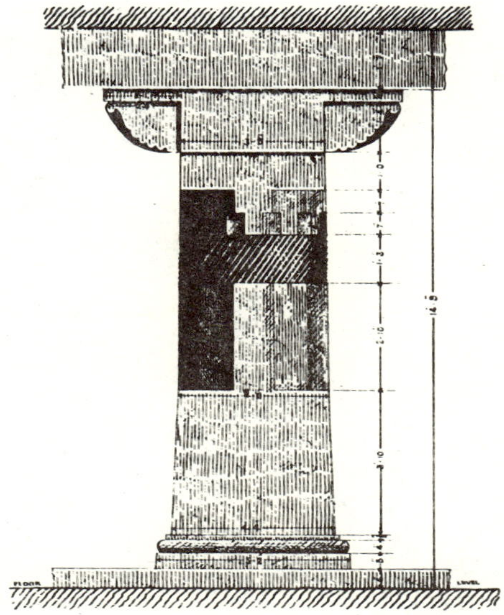

C

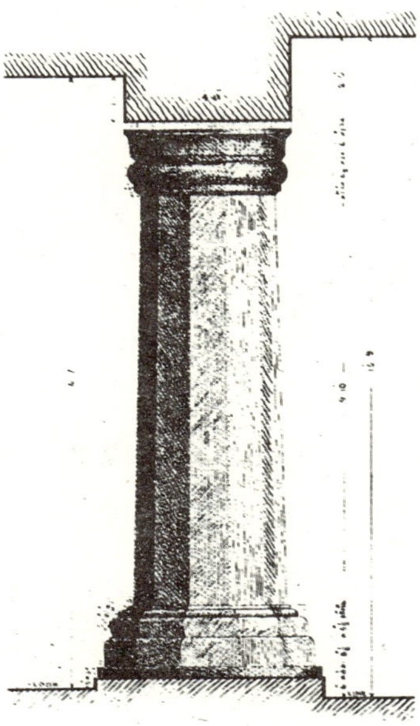

D

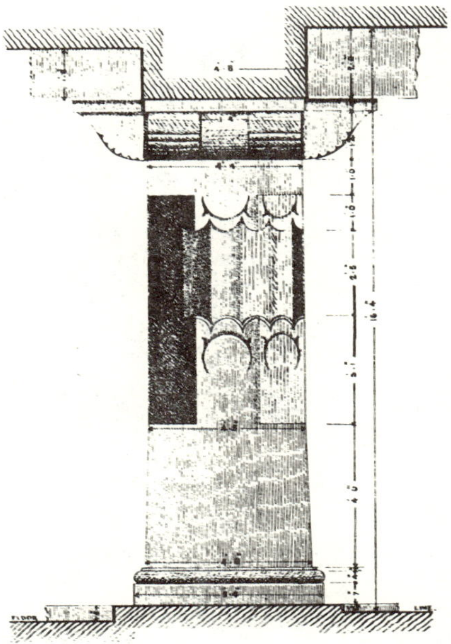

E

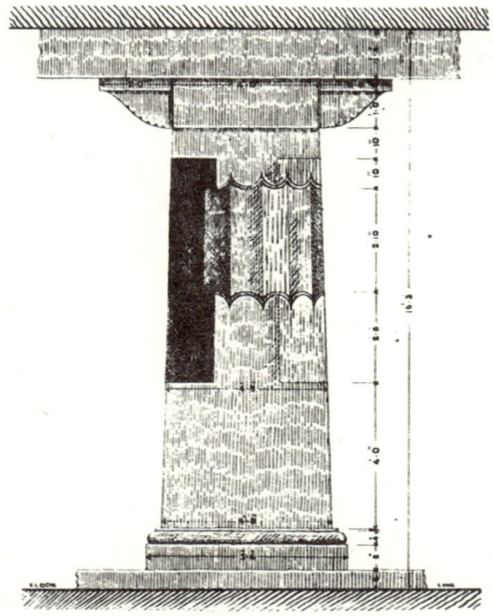

F

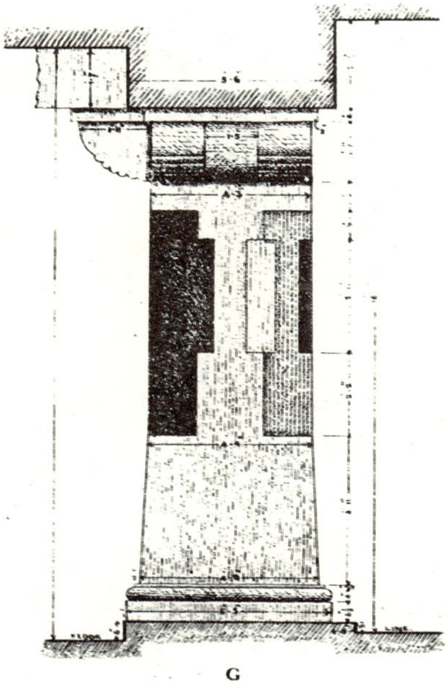

G

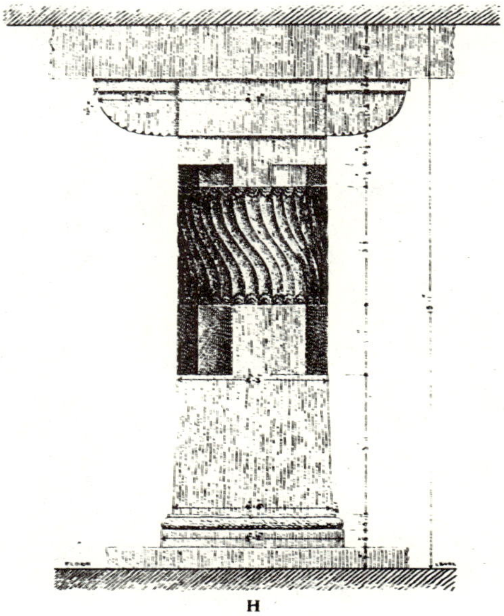

H

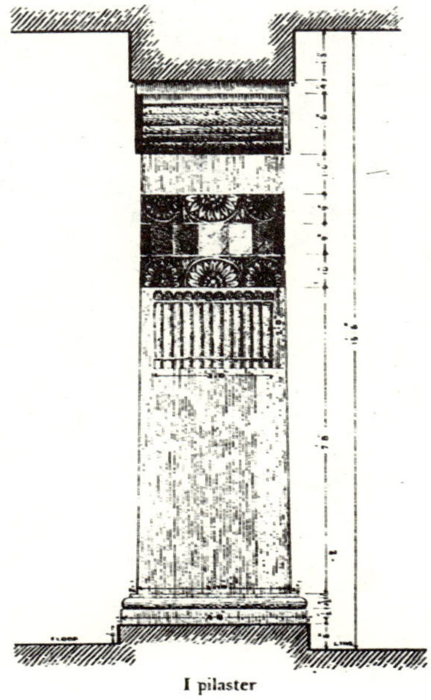

I pilaster

Pillars and Pilasters in Cave 2

a. CORNER VIEW OF INTERIOR OF CAVE 2

b. SIDE VIEW OF INTERIOR OF CAVE 2

a. CENTRAL VIEW OF INTERIOR OF CAVE 2

b. INTERIOR VIEW OF INTERIOR OF CAVE 5

a. Images of the Buddha and his attendants, Bodhisattvas, on right wall of Vestibule of Cave 2

b. Images of the Buddha and attendants on left wall of Vestibule of Cave 2

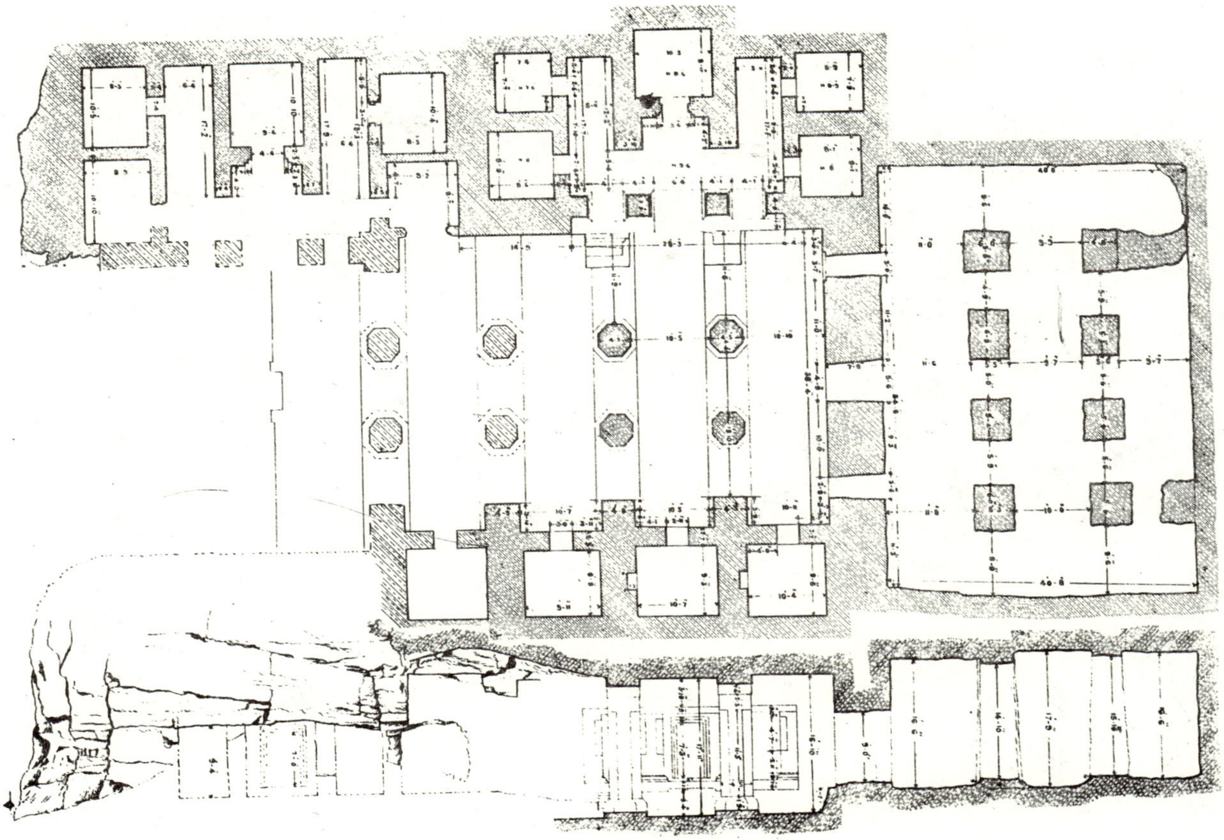

c. Cross section of Cave 3

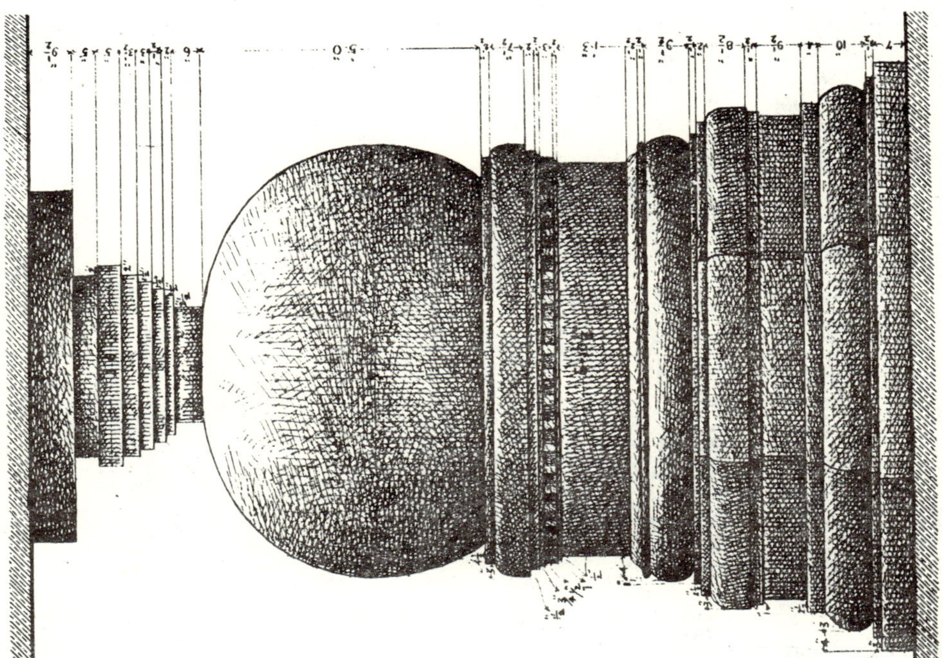

d. Stupa in Cave 2

a. Portico in Interior of Cave 4

b

a

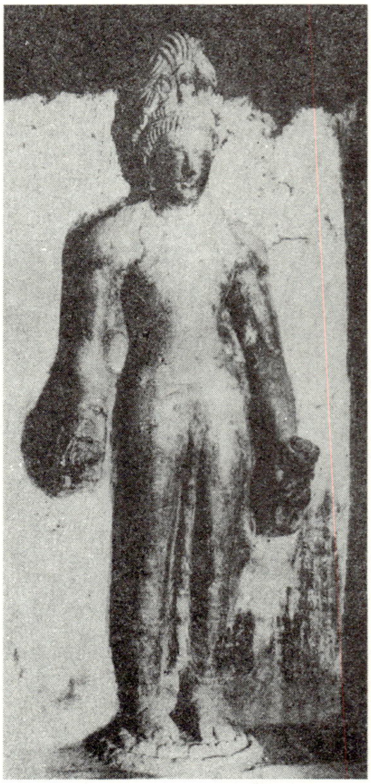

c

Stupa and Bodhisattvas in Cave 2

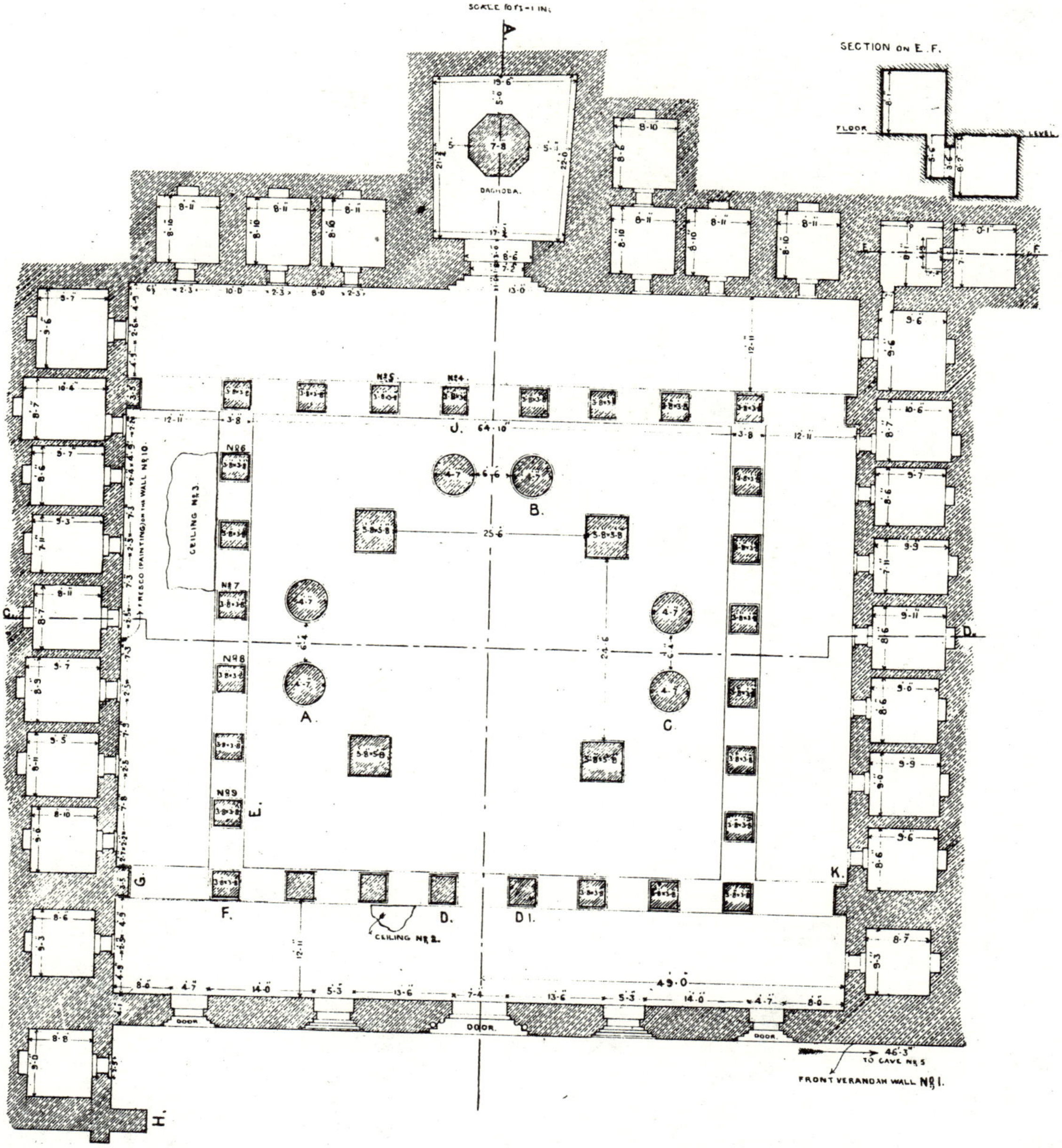

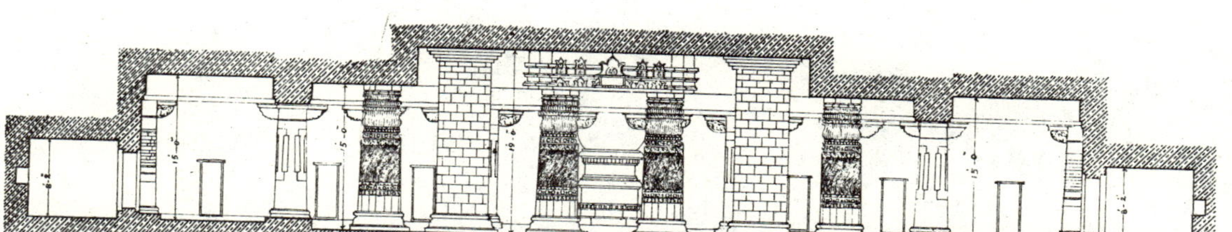

PLAN AND SECTIONS OF CAVE 4

a. Facade of Cave 5 from N.E.

b. Facade of Cave 4 from N.W.

c. General View of Caves 4, 5 and 6

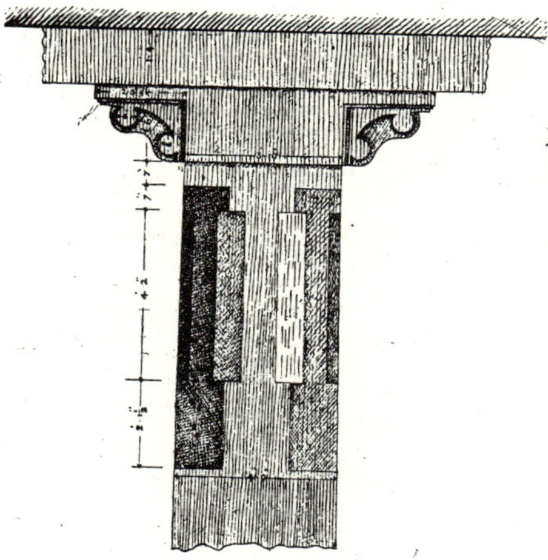

Detail of pillar J, showing brackets

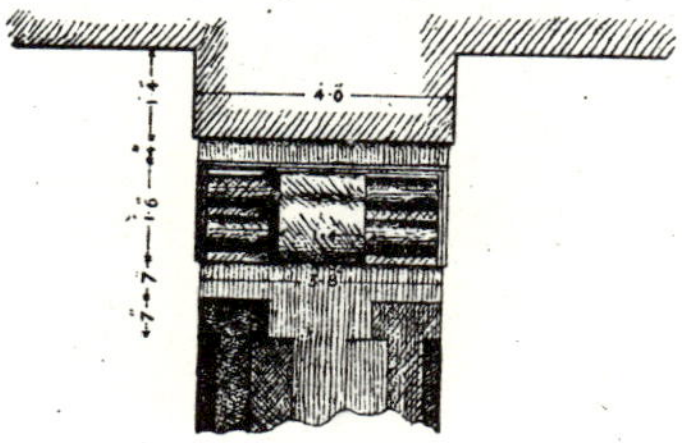

Side view of above

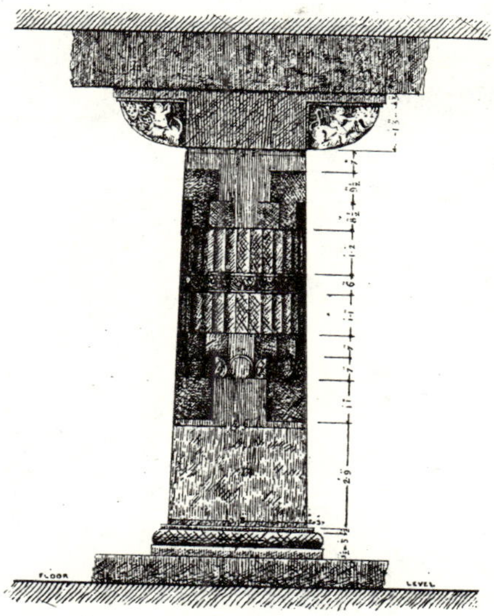

Detail of pillar D

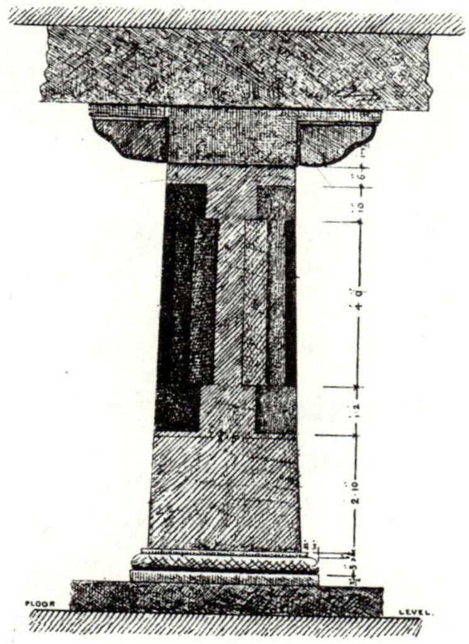

Detail of pillar F

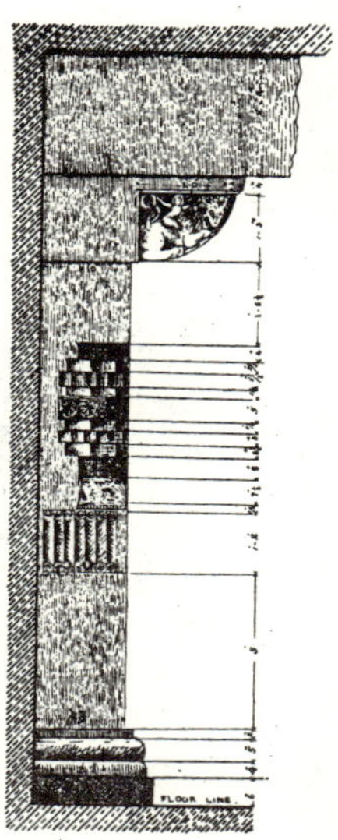

Side of pilaster G

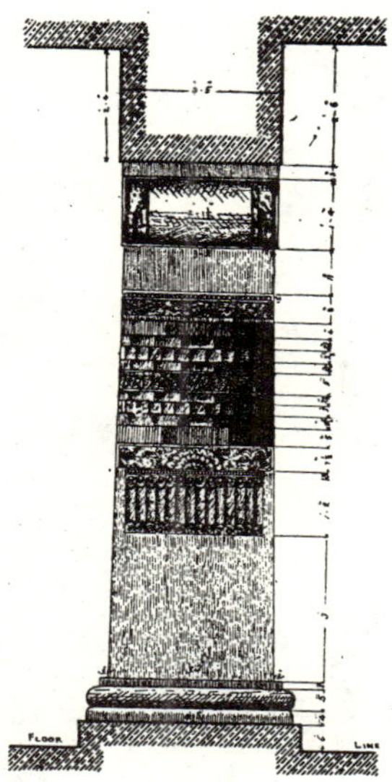

Detail of pilaster G

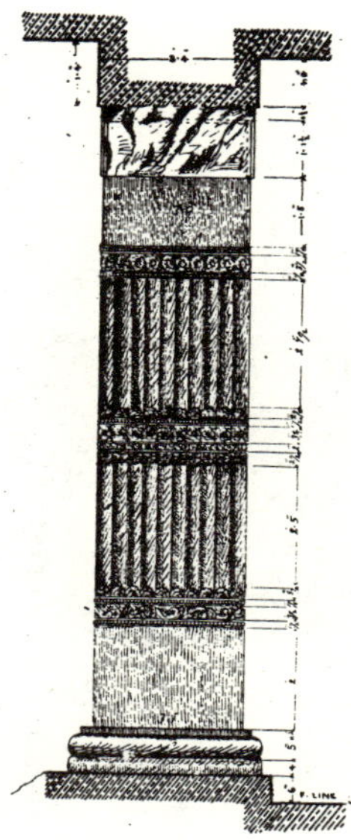

Detail of pilaster H

PILLARS AND PILASTERS IN CAVE 4

a. PILLAR BRACKET IN CAVE 4

b. UPPER PART OF PRINCIPAL DOORWAY OF CAVE 4

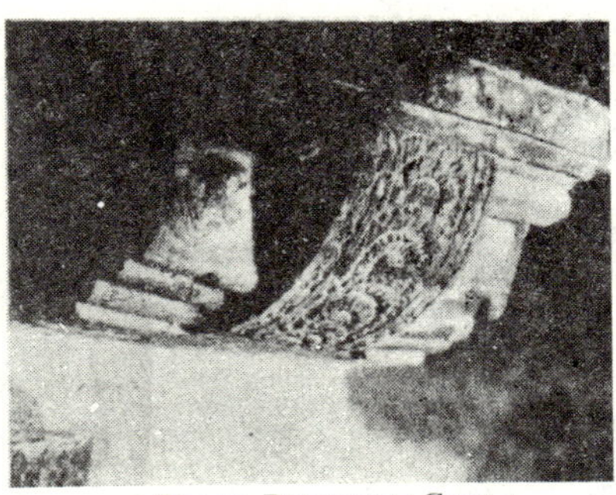

c. PILLAR BRACKET IN CAVE 4

c. PILASTER IN INTERIOR OF CAVE 4

d. PILLAR BRACKET IN CAVE 4

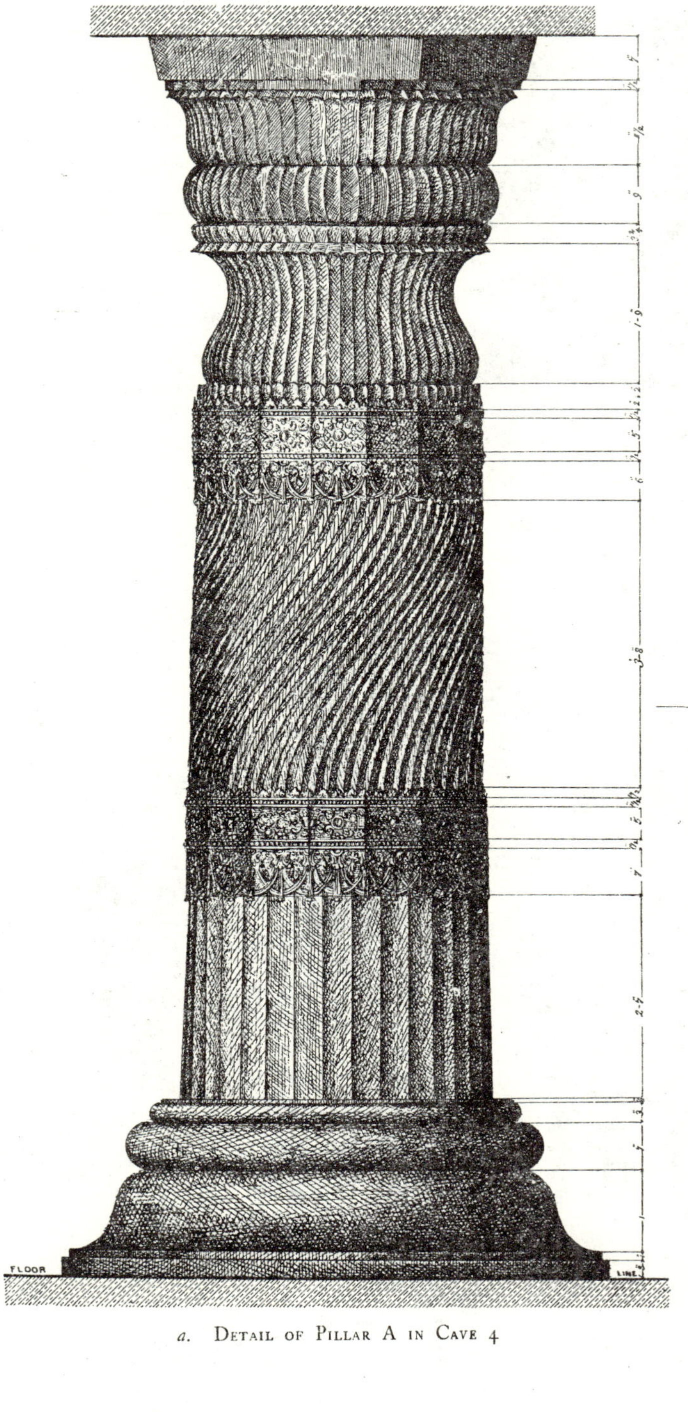

a. Detail of Pillar A in Cave 4

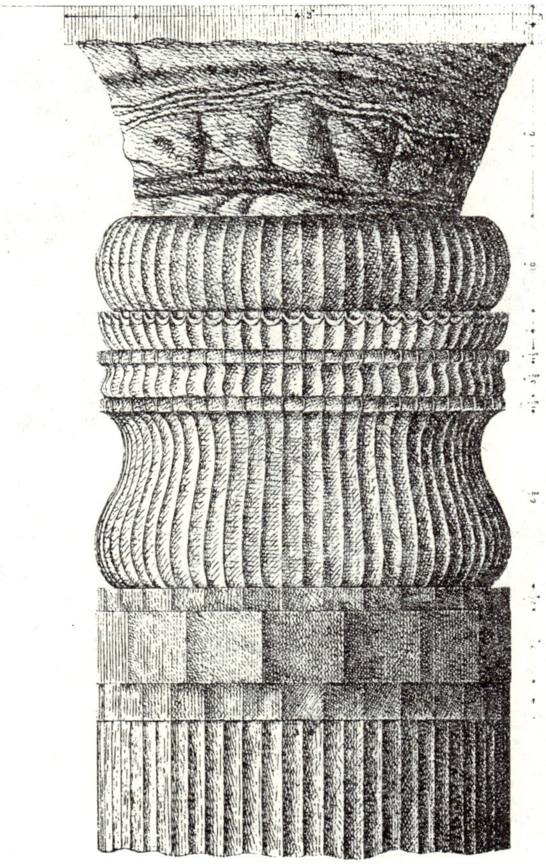

b

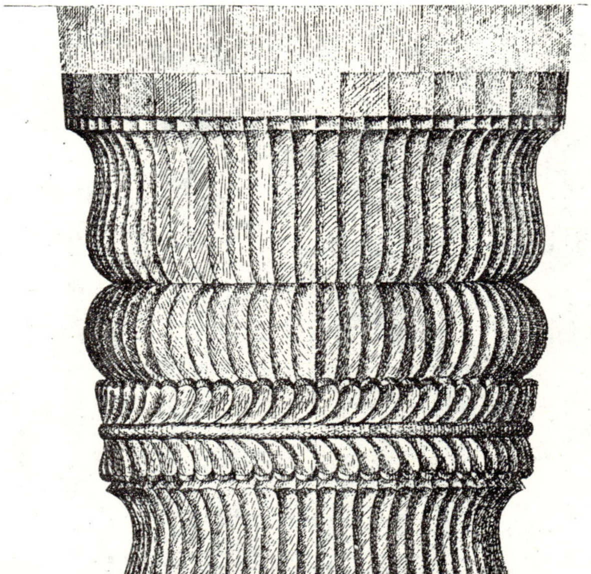

c

b. & *c.* Details of Pillars in Cave 4

Inner face of pillar E

Outer face of pillar E

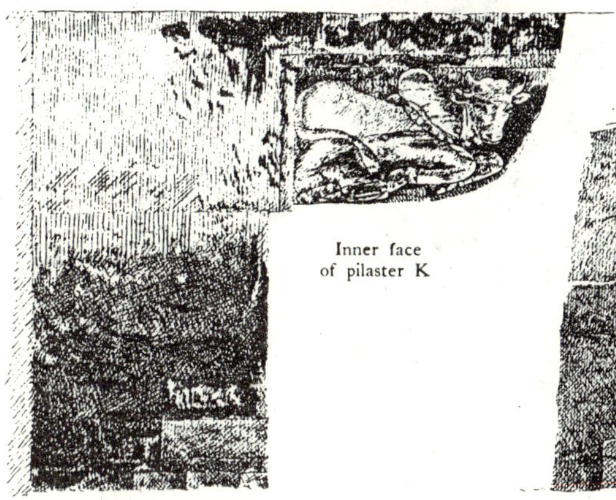

Inner face of pilaster K

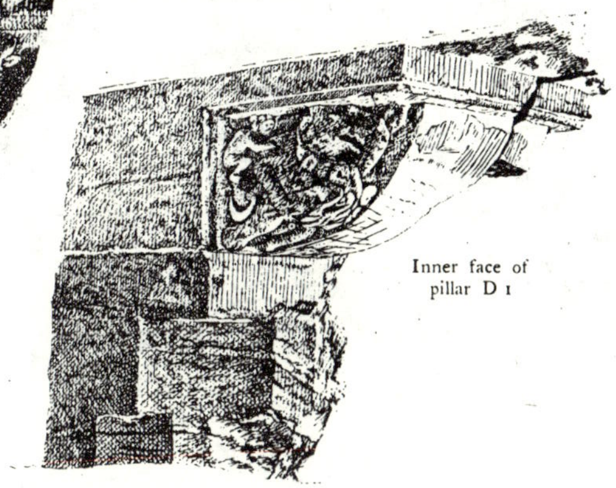

Inner face of pillar D 1

Inner face of pillar D

Outer face of pillar D

PILLAR BRACKETS IN CAVE 4

PLATE XV

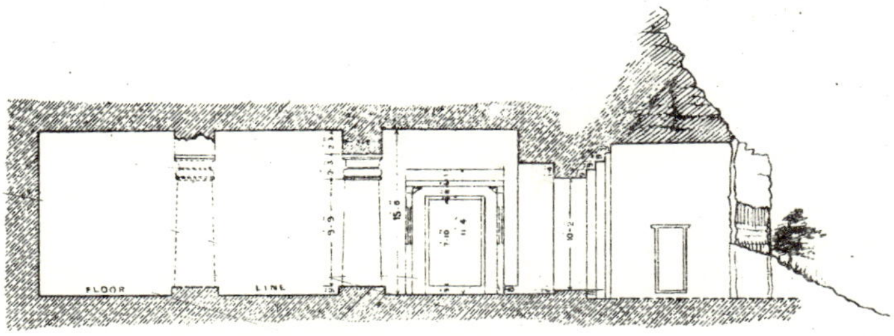

a. Cross section of Cave 5

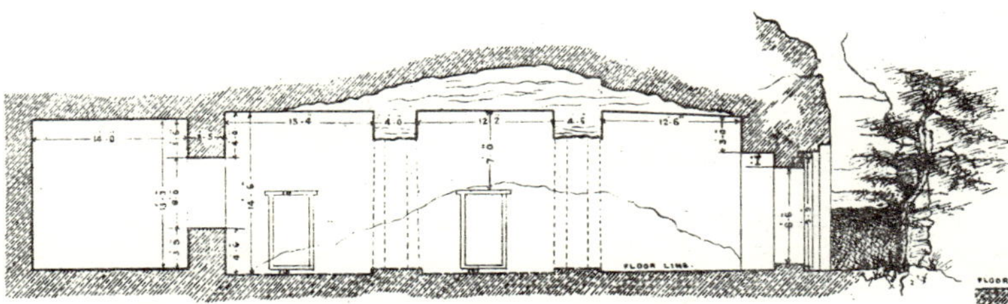

b. Cross section of Cave 6

c. Pillar in Cave 5

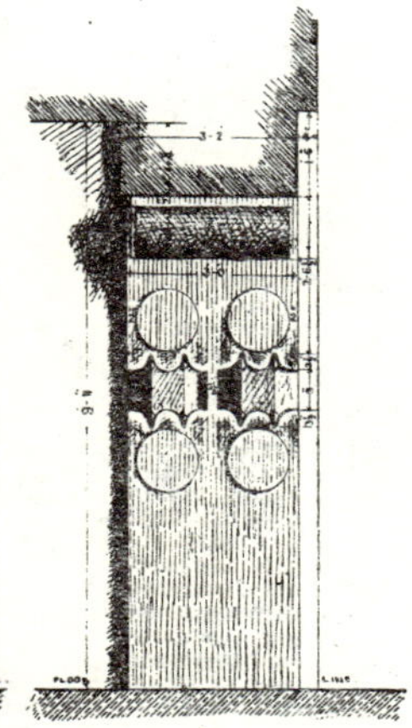

d. Detail of pilaster A in Cave 6

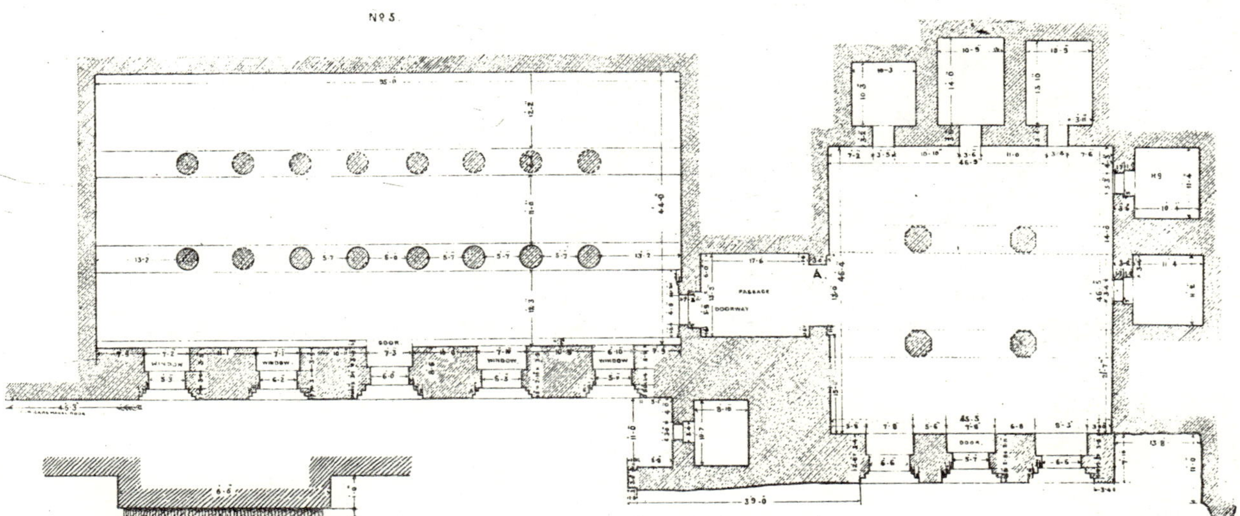

e. Plan of Caves 5 and 6

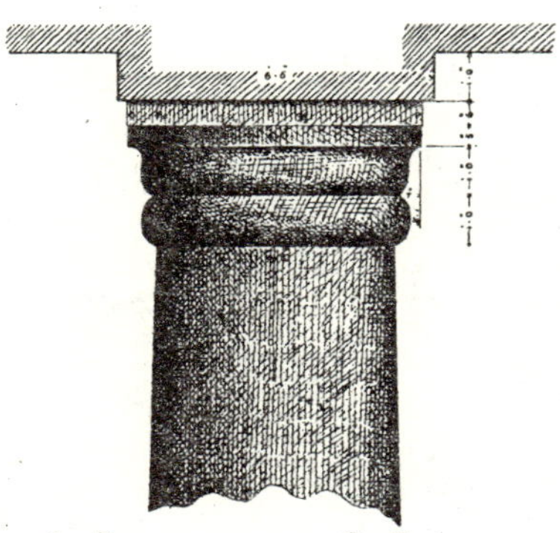

f. Detail of pillar C, Cave 7

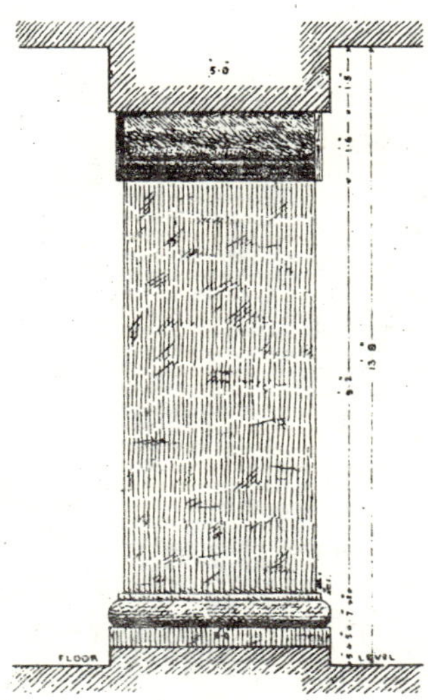

h. Detail of pillar A, Cave 7

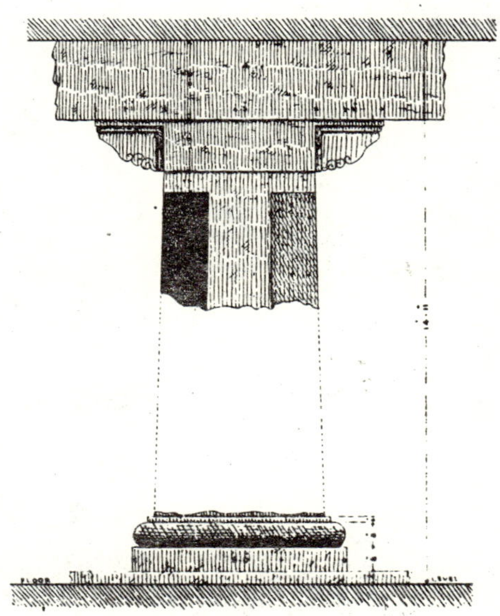

i. Detail of pillar B, Cave 7

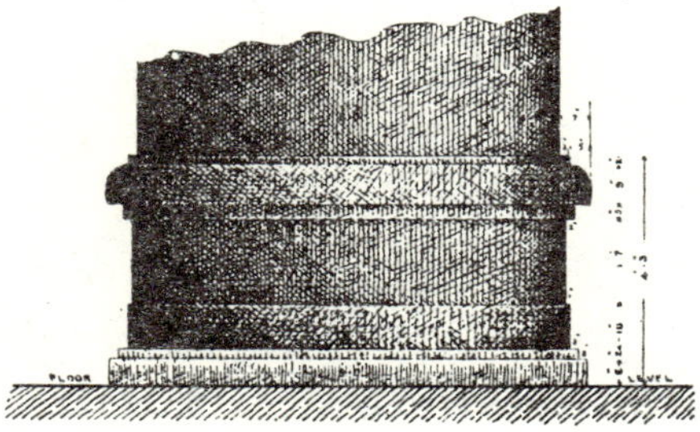

g. Detail of stupa D, Cave 7

PLATE XVI

Ceiling and Wall Decorations in Cave 4

PLATE XVII

PILLAR AND WALL DECORATIONS IN CAVE 4

Wall Decorations in Cave 4

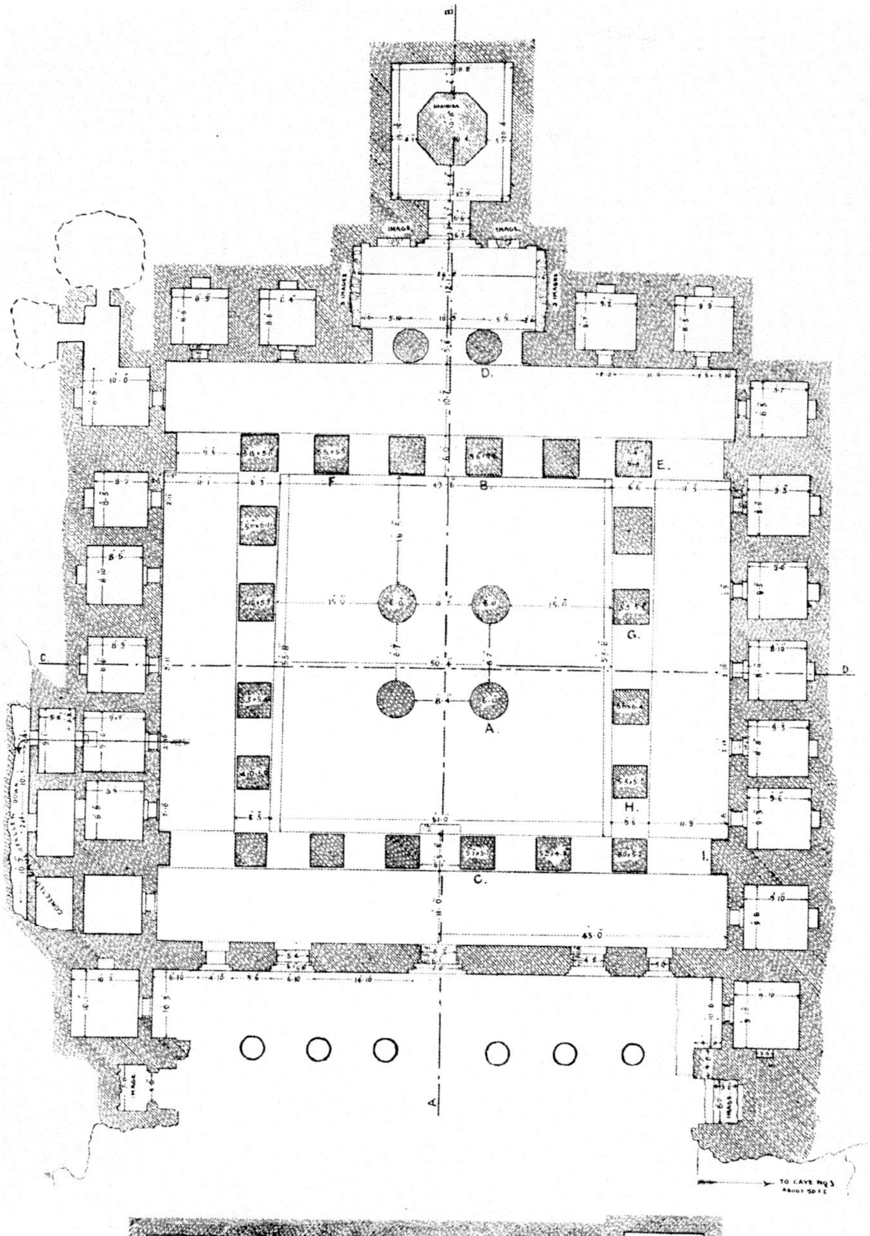

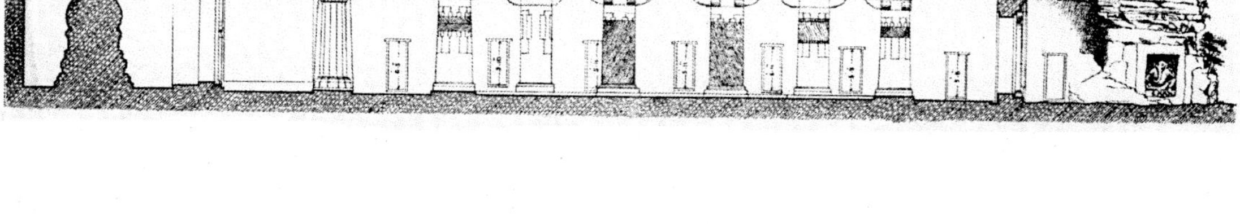

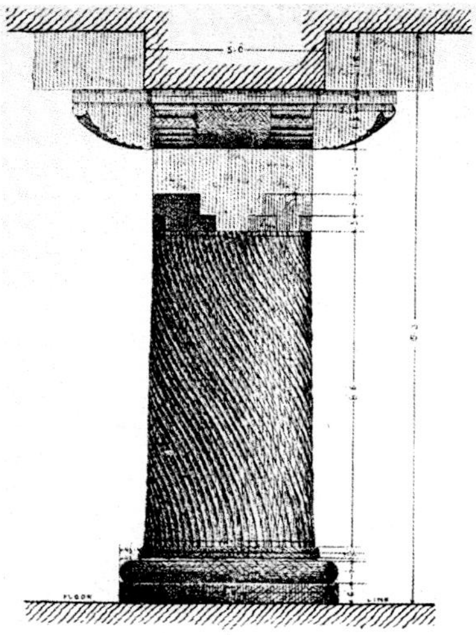
A

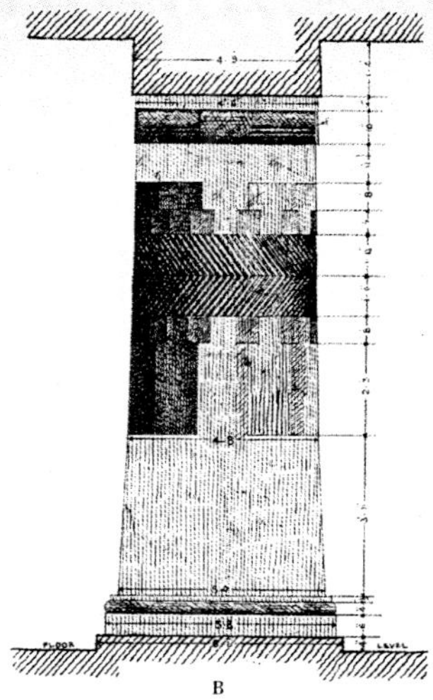
B

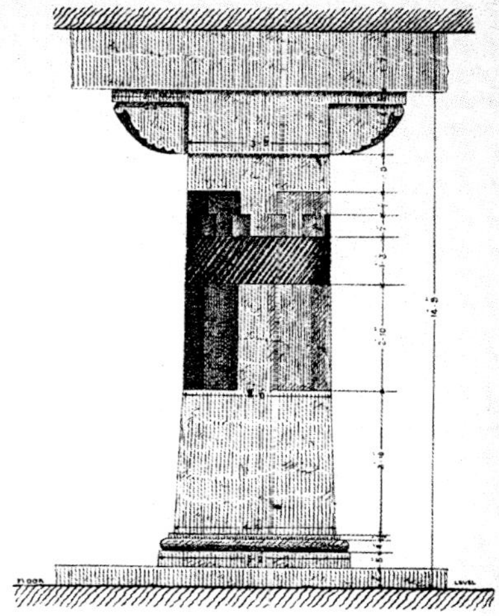
C

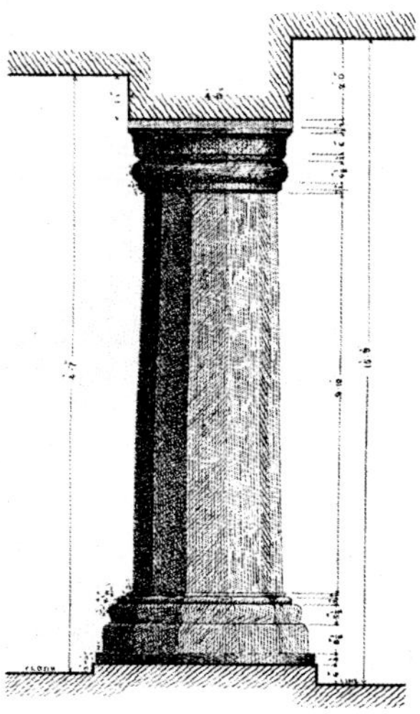
D

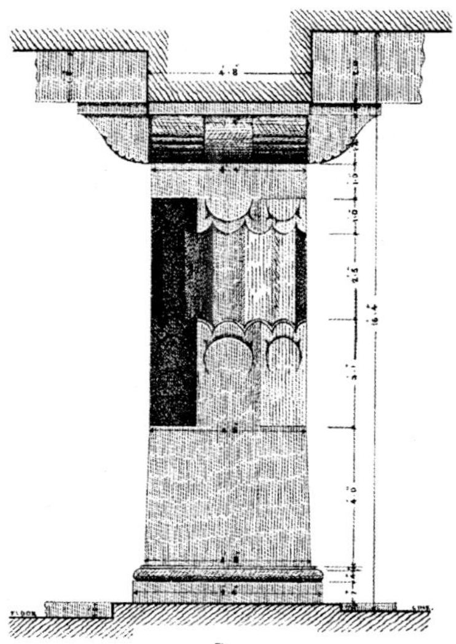
E

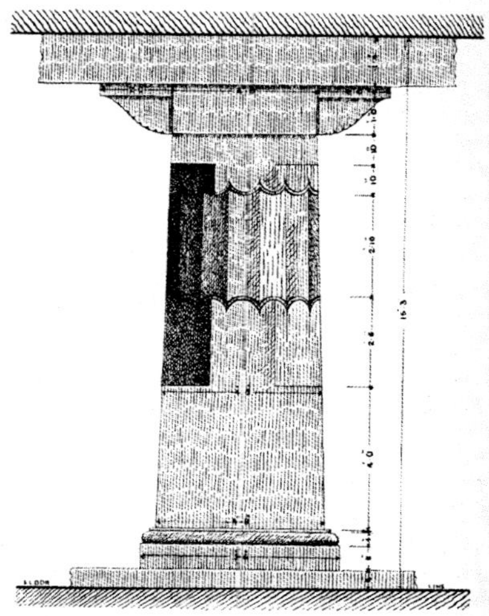
F

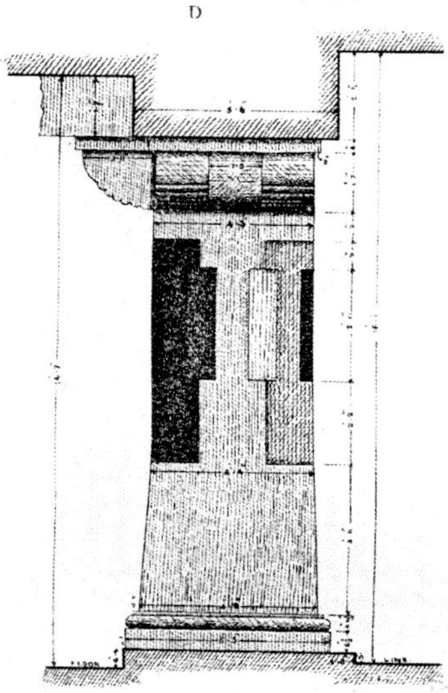
G

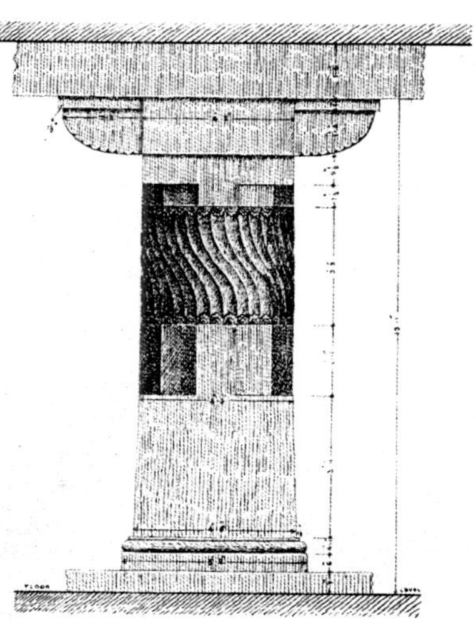
H

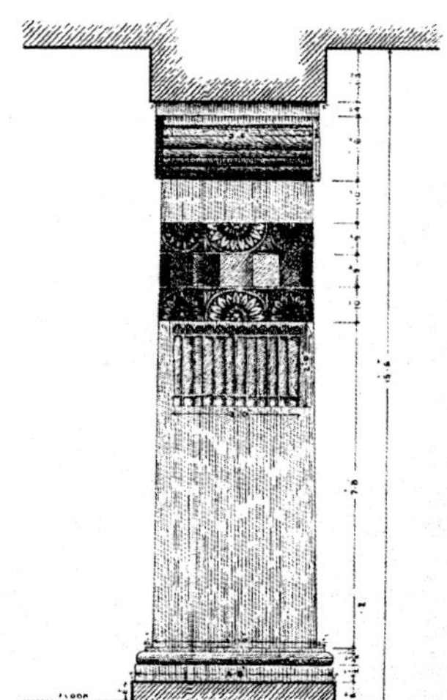
I pilaster

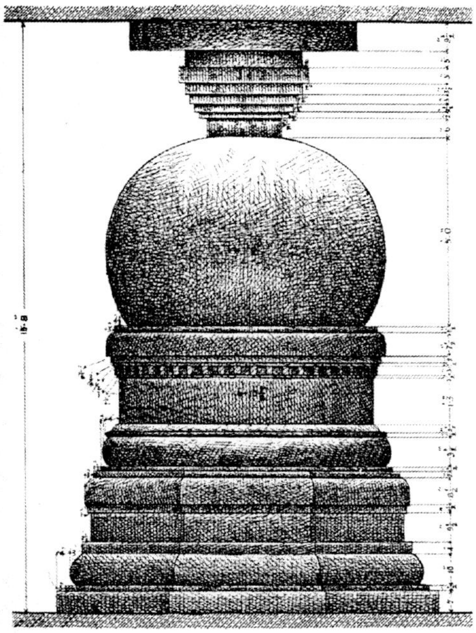

a. Stupa in Cave 2

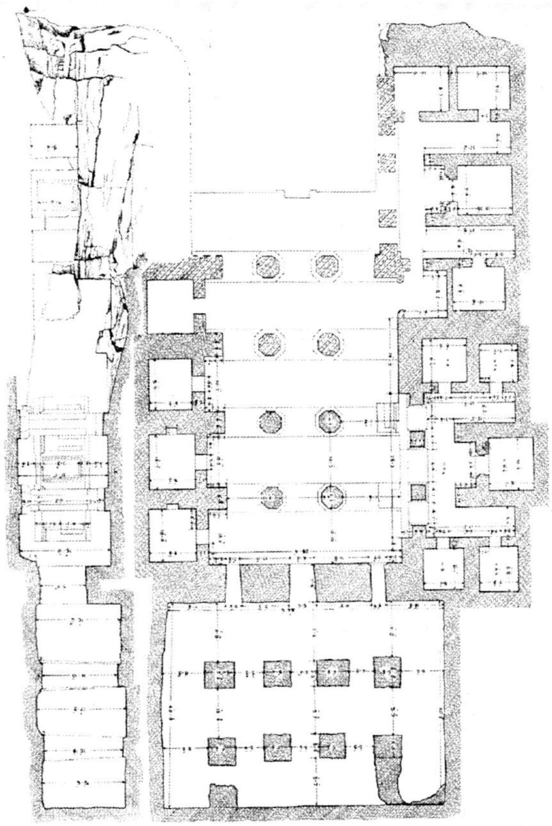

c. Cross section of Cave 3

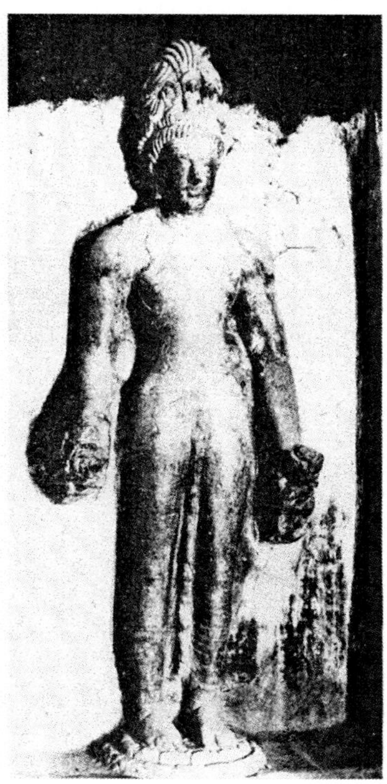

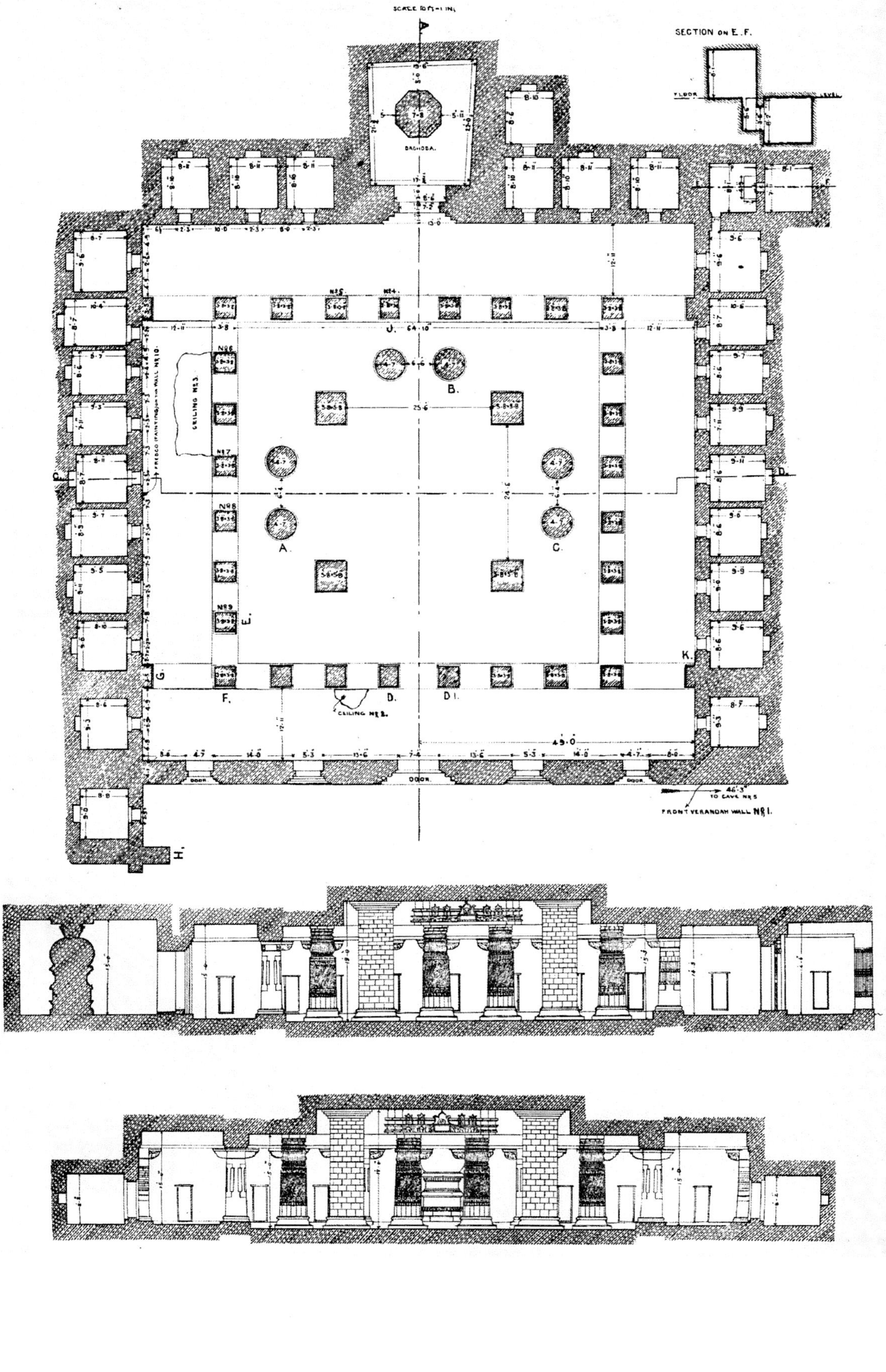
SECTION ON E.F.
DAGHOBA.
CEILING Nº 3.
CEILING Nº 2.
FRONT VERANDAH WALL Nº 1.
TO CAVE Nº 5
DOOR.

b. Façade of Cave 4 from N.W.

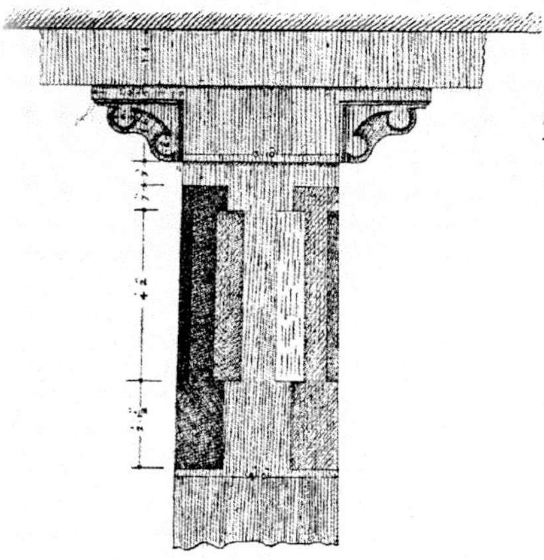

Detail of pillar J, showing brackets

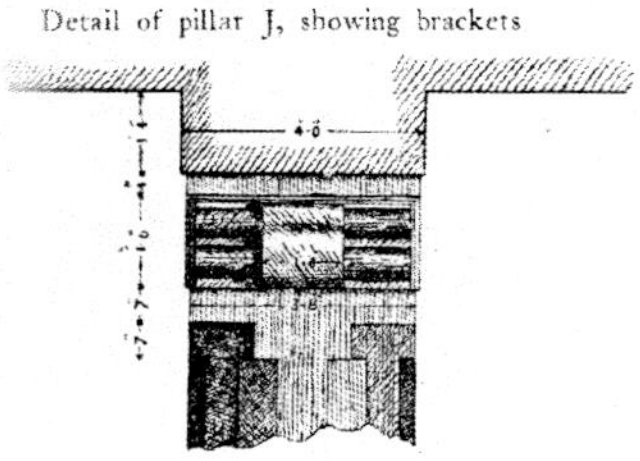

Side view of above

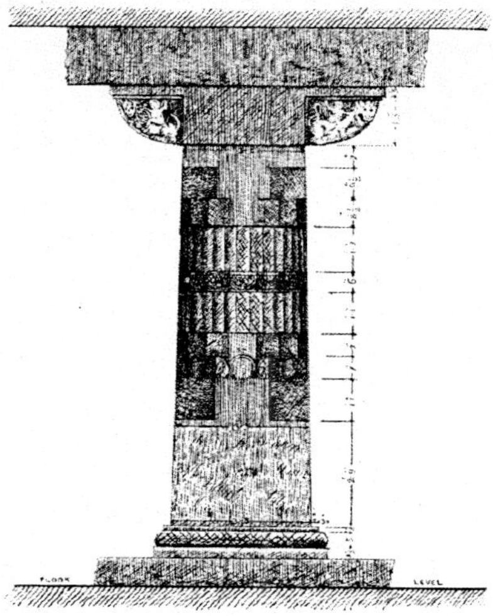

Detail of pillar D

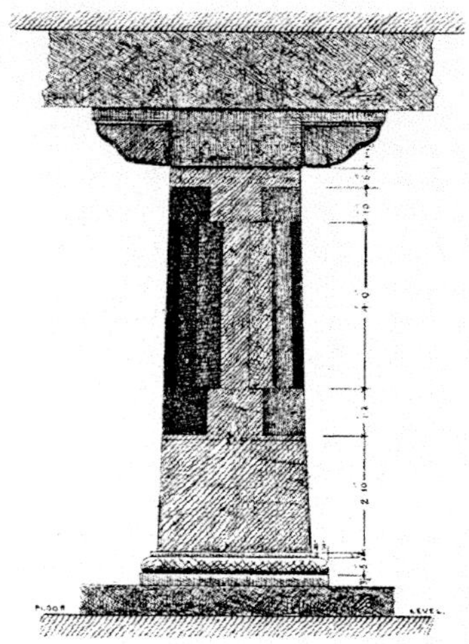

Detail of pillar F

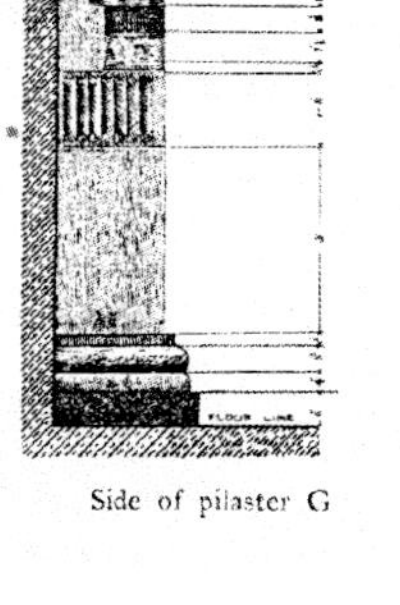

Side of pilaster G

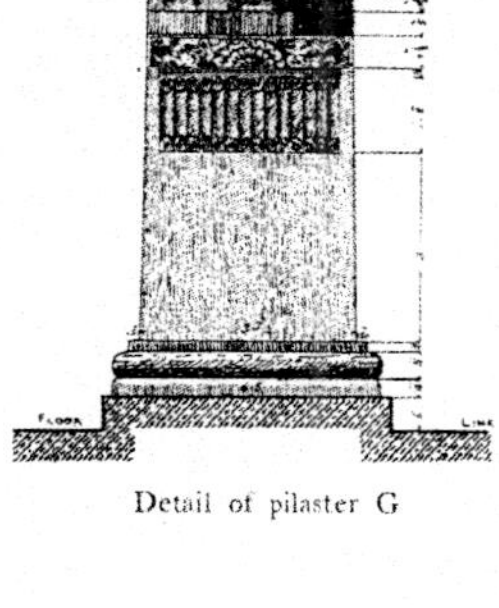

Detail of pilaster G

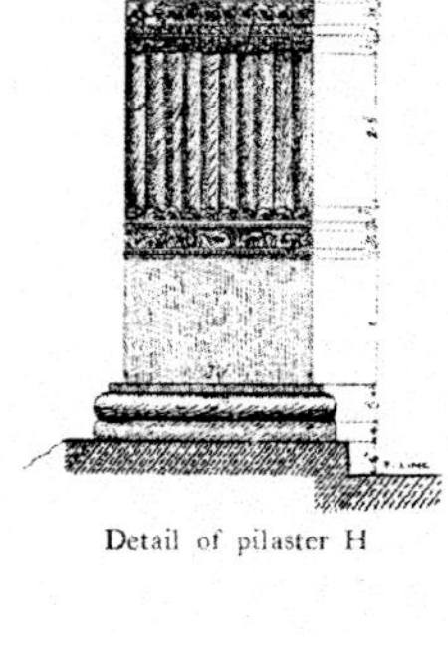

Detail of pilaster H

c. Pillar Bracket in Cave 4

e. Pilaster in Interior of Cave 4

d. Pillar Bracket in Cave 4

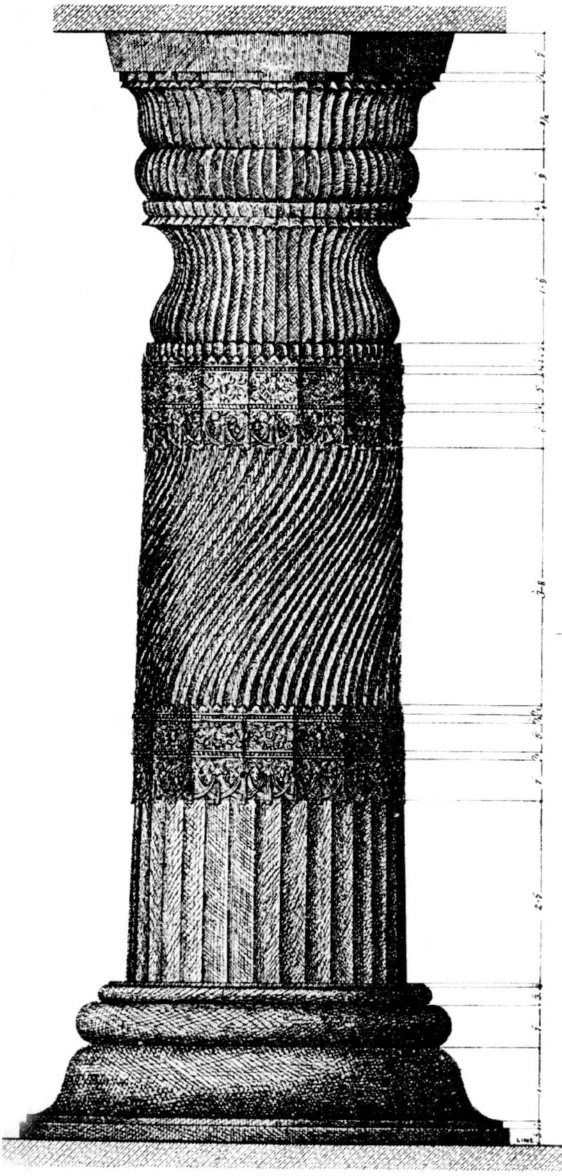

a. DETAIL OF PILLAR A IN CAVE 4

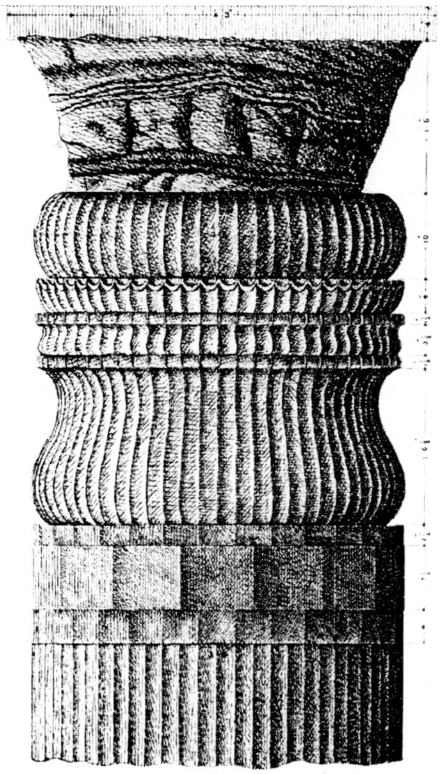

b

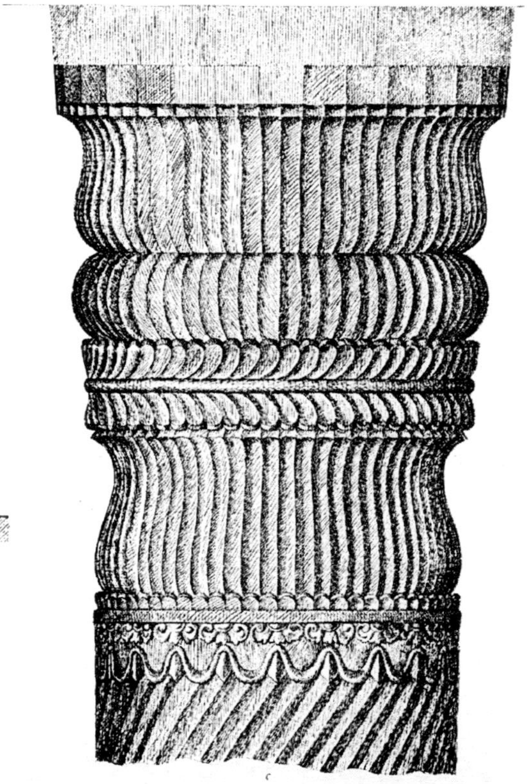

c

Inner face of pillar E

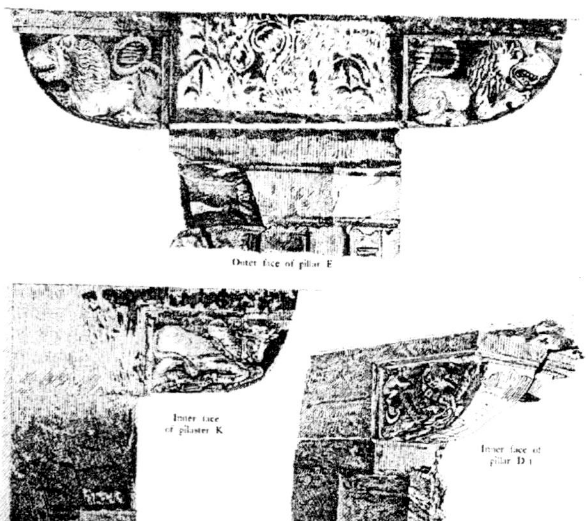

Outer face of pillar E

Inner face of pilaster K

Inner face of pillar D 1

Inner face of pillar D

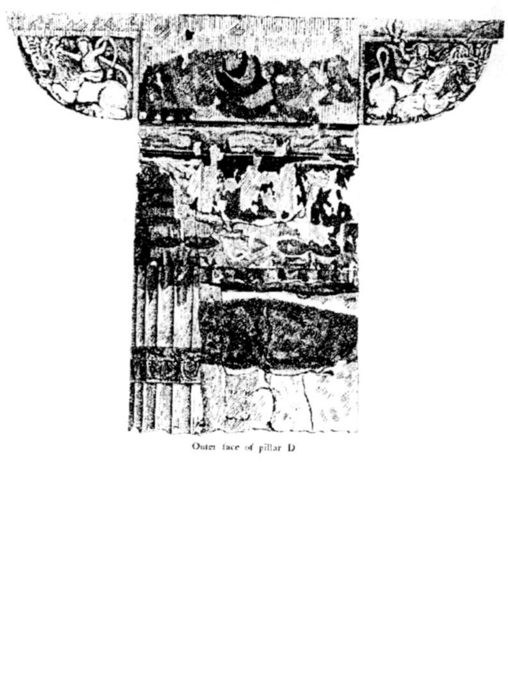

Outer face of pillar D

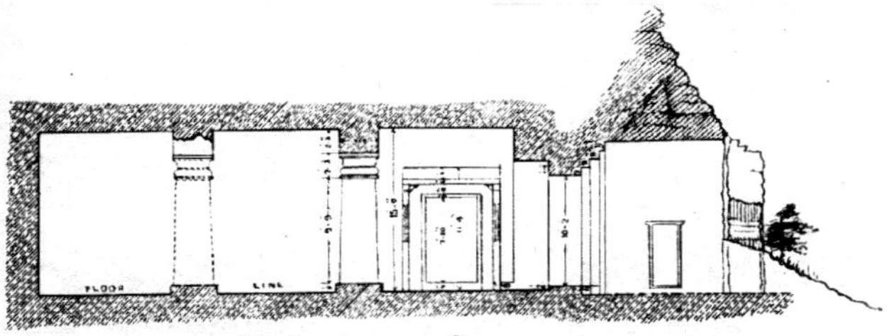

a. Cross section of Cave 5

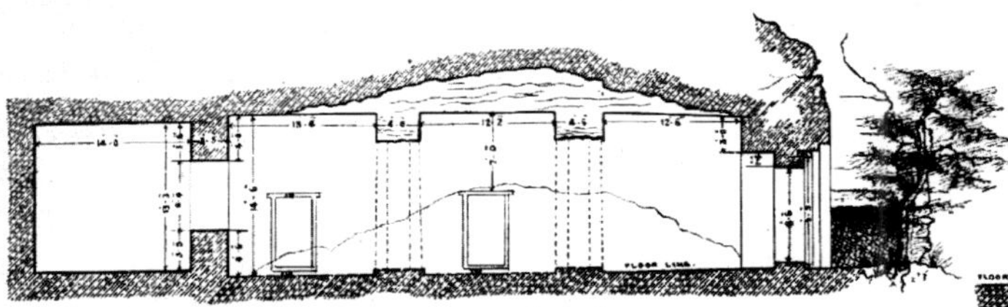

b. Cross section of Cave 6

c. Pillar in Cave 5

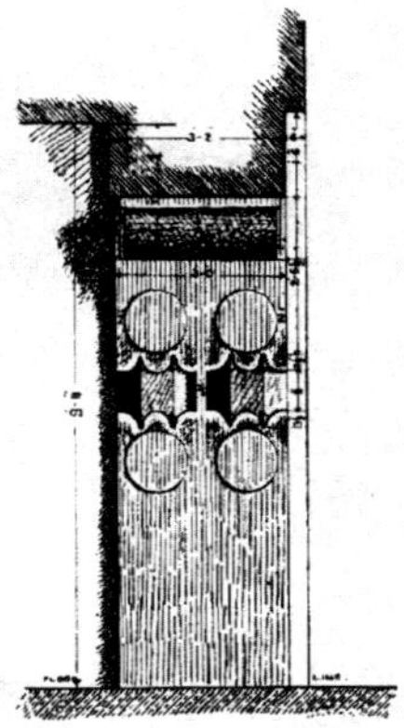

d. Detail of pilaster A in Cave 6

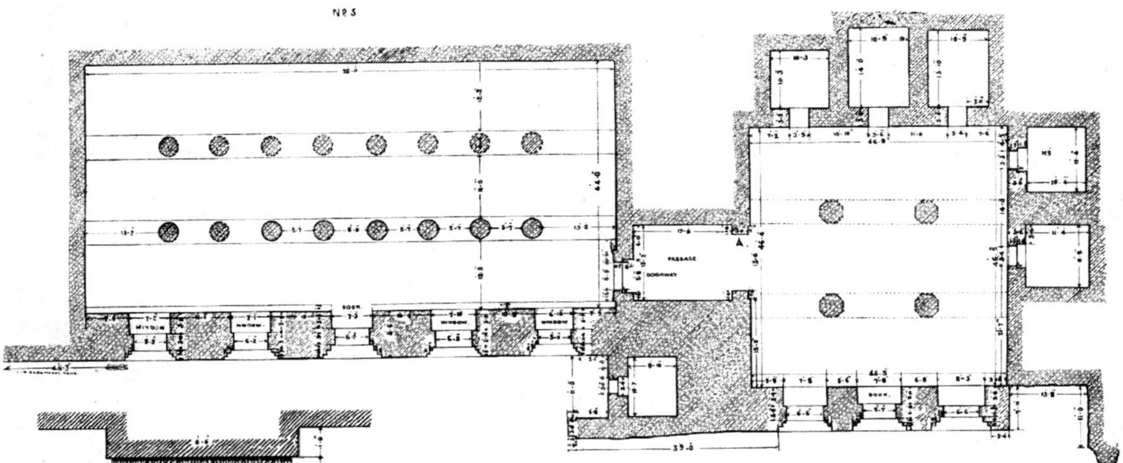

e. Plan of Caves 5 and 6

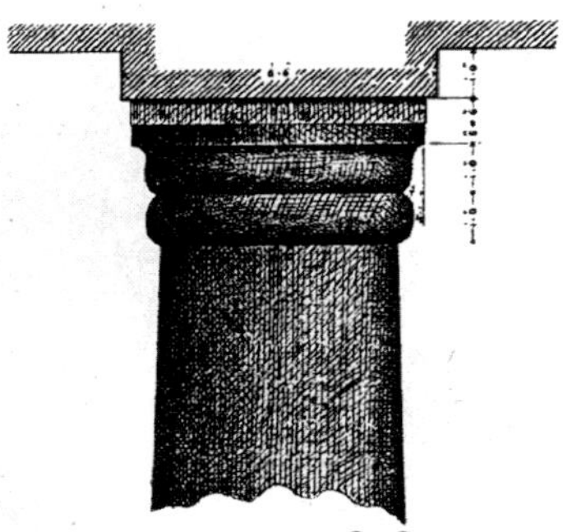

f. Detail of pillar C, Cave 7

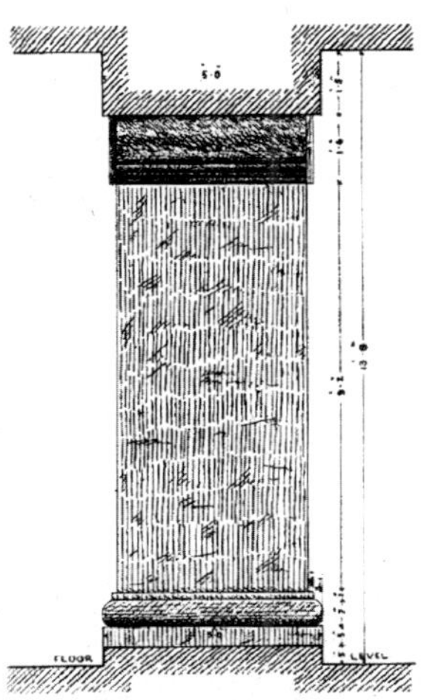

h. Detail of pillar A, Cave 7

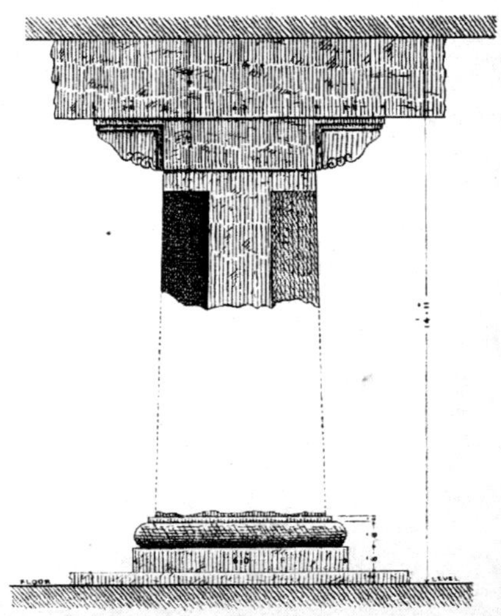

i. Detail of pillar B, Cave 7

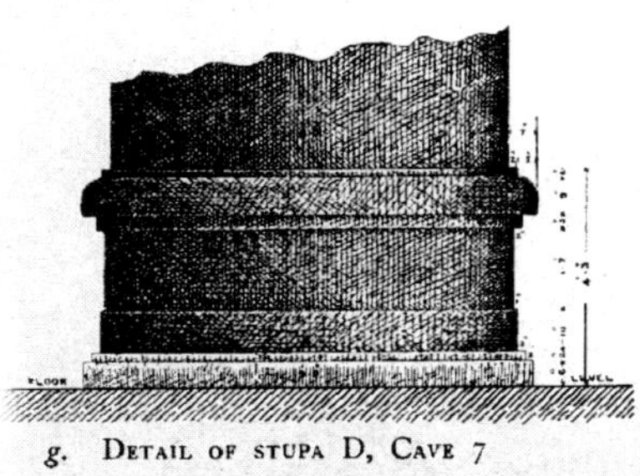

g. Detail of stupa D, Cave 7

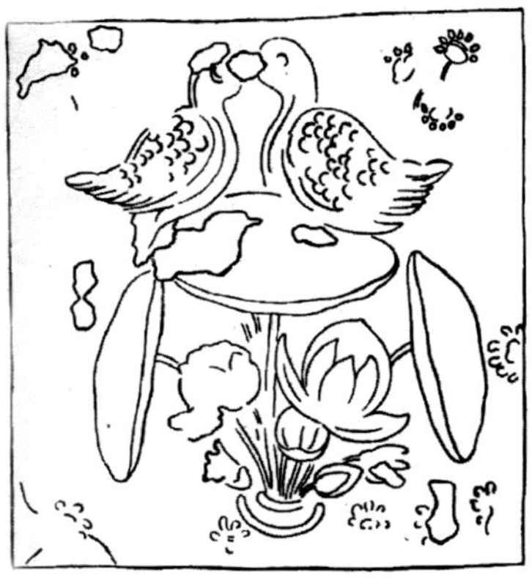

PILLAR AND WALL DECORATIONS IN CAVE 4

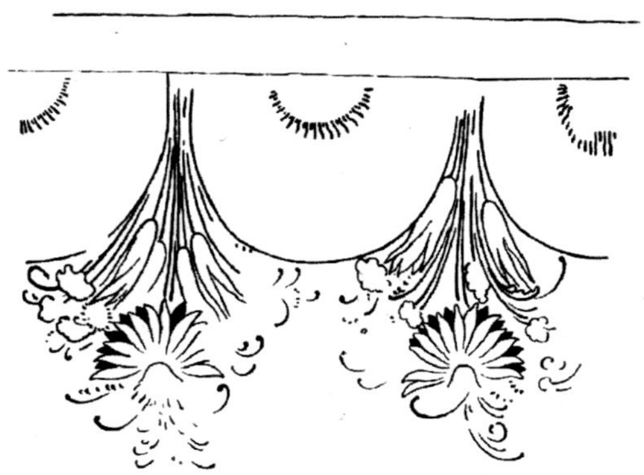

KEY TO THE COLOUR PLATES
Bagh Caves (published by the Medici Society)

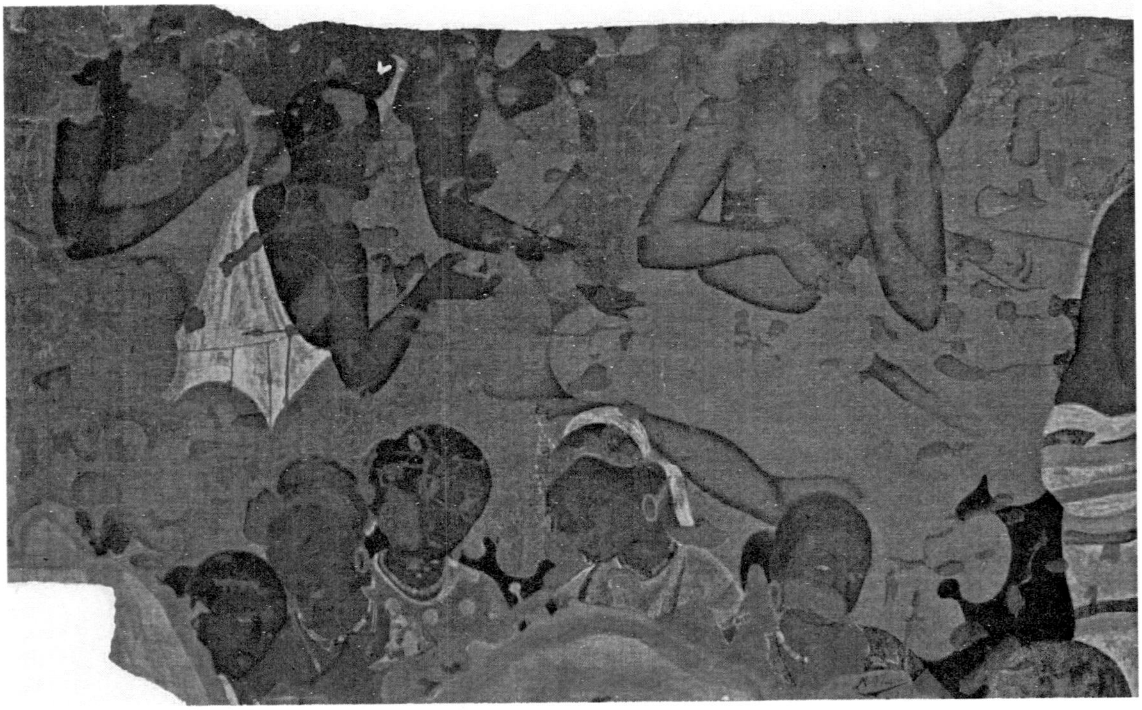

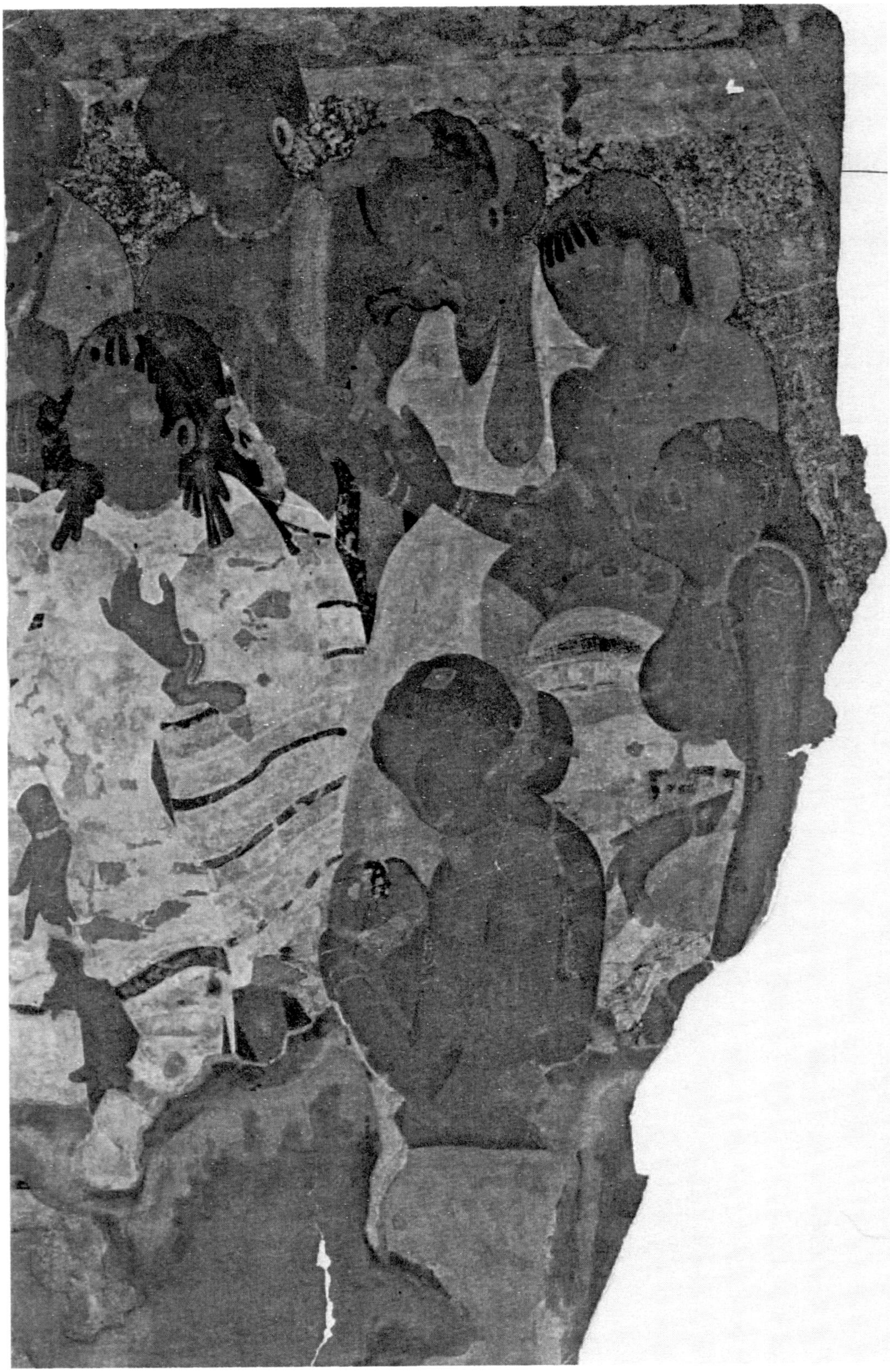

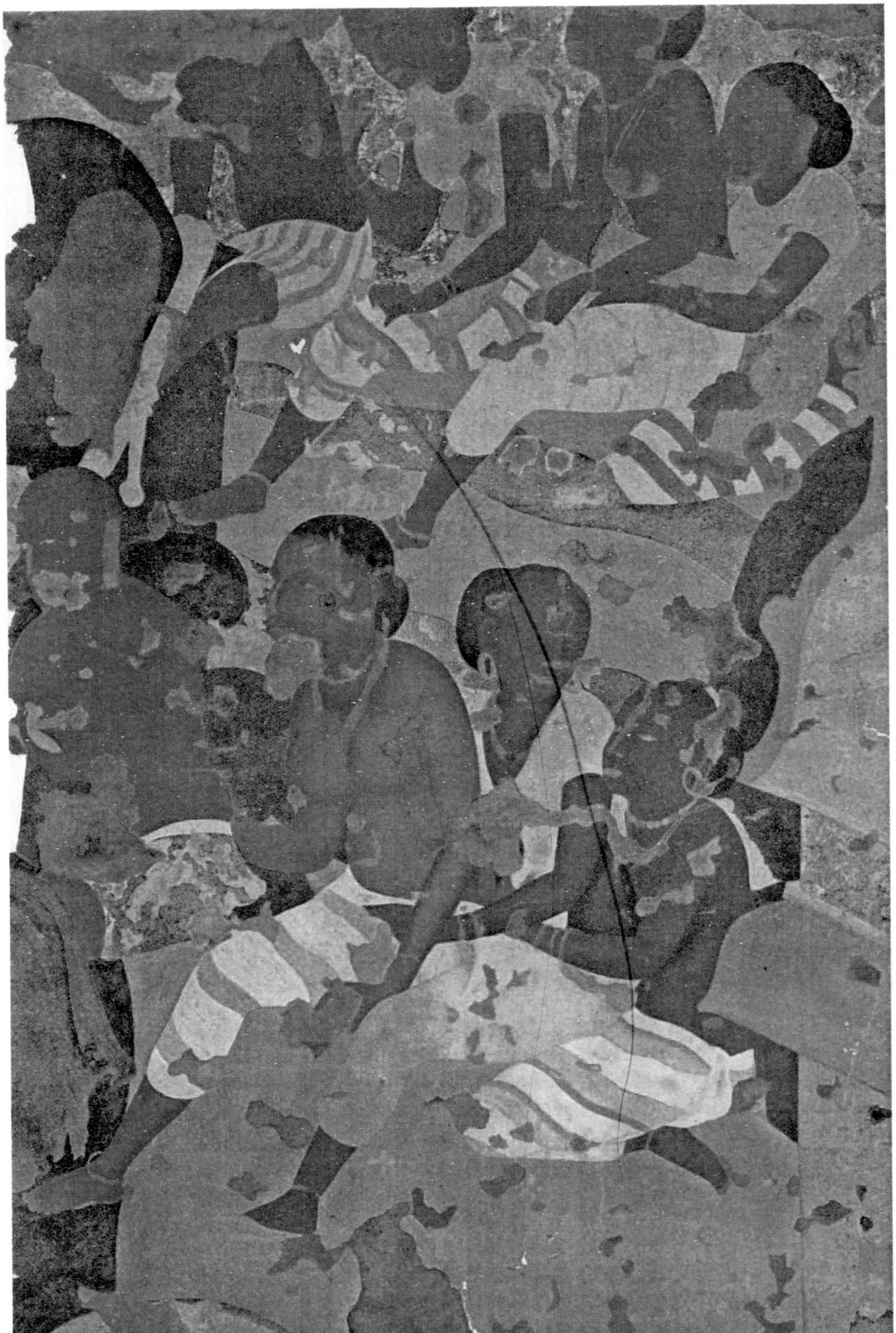